Imi

Imi

A LIFETIME IN THE DAYS
OF THE FAMILY MANDEL

Terry Fred Horowitz

LIBRARY *of the*
HOLOCAUST
Washington, D.C.

Printed in the United States of America
ISBN: 978-1882326-13-6
Library of Congress Control Number: 2017954609

Library of the Holocaust Foundation
PO Box 1651
Silver Spring, Maryland 20915
(800) 651-9350
www.LibraryoftheHolocaust.org

Contents

Preface / vii

Chapter One / 1

Chapter Two / 9

Chapter Three / 21

Chapter Four / 39

Chapter Five /59

Chapter Six / 73

Chapter Seven / 85

Chapter Eight / 95

Chapter Nine / 103

Chapter Ten / 109

Chapter Eleven /123

Epilogue / 127

Selected Bibliography /153

Preface

In 1993, four years after the Communist state in Hungary was dismantled and two years after the last Soviet troops were withdrawn from that country, effectively ending the Warsaw Pact, my wife, Judy, and I, and another couple with their daughter, visited Czechoslovakia, Hungary and Poland. Over a period of two weeks we made a pilgrimage to five former concentration camps—Theresienstadt, Treblinka, Auschwitz, Birkenau (Auschwitz II), and Majdanek.

We knew that at Auschwitz-Birkenau, on the outskirts of Oswiecim, and Southwest of Cracow, Poland, we would be visiting the largest killing center in the entire Nazi universe. Of the approximately 2,000,000 Jews killed there, in the summer of 1944, 437,402 of them had been deported from Hungary. While there, we saw the railroad track leading to gate with the mocking sign, *Arbeit Mach Frei* (work makes you free), the elevated watch towers, the few remaining barracks, the blown-up remnants of the crematoria, the rooms used for "experimentation," plus stacks of shoes, glasses, and luggage. At one point, while we were saying a silent prayer, a nearby group of Polish teenagers romped about, yelling at one another, oblivious to the historical nature of our environs.

At Treblinka, about fifty miles northeast of Warsaw, we saw concrete blocks, symbolically marking the path of the former railway line, and the seventeen thousand stones, each one representing a Jewish town or city, the population of which was exterminated at the camp.

At Theresienstadt, forty miles Northwest of Prague, in the Czech Republic, we explored the quintessential propaganda camp, which hid a more sinister purpose. In reality, this "beautified" ghetto had been a collection center for deportations for forced labor, or more likely, to extermination camps. Of the 140,000 Jews transferred to Theresienstadt, 90,000 were "deported," to their deaths, while of the remaining 50,000, 33,000 died there.

But, it was Majdanek, overlooking the Polish town of Lublin, that had the most lasting and devastating impact on me. It was still in "pristine" condition—barbed wire (electrical fence), guard towers, crematorium, gas chamber, dissection table, and shoes of camp victims. One estimate (Russian) surmised that no less than 400,000 Jews had been put to their death there. While walking toward an open field in which thousands of these victims had been burned, covered with lime, and then buried in mass graves, I stumbled upon a large white object, which, according to my doctor companion, was part of a human pelvis! It had been there for over fifty years.

In Martin Gilbert's book, *Atlas of the Holocaust*, his estimates are listed by region and country. By my count, 5,352, 349 Jews were murdered between 1 September 1939 and 8 May 1945.

My father's parents came from Brest-Litovsk, my mother's from Minsk, in present-day Belarus. Both cities were in the so-called "Pale of Settlement," which, throughout history, had gone back and forth from Russian to Polish jurisdiction. Brest-Litovsk is 125 miles from Warsaw, Minsk, 290 miles from the Polish capital. All four grandparents immigrated to the United States in 1905. According to Martin Gilbert's count, from June 22, 1941 to October 31, 1942, 30,000 Jews were deported and massacred in Brest-Litovsk (in two major incursions), while 48,218 Jews were murdered in Minsk (in seven incidences) from June 22, 1941 to October 21, 1943. One can't help but think about the relatives and friends of my grandparents surely among the victims.

While in Budapest, we visited the house of a Jewish artist who had survived the war for two horrifying years, hiding out in his basement atelier (which he showed us), supported by his gentile neighbors, who gave him and his family fair warning when either Nazis or the despicable, "home-grown" hoodlums of the Arrow Cross party approached the complex. As a parting gesture, our Hungarian artist friend gave us a small golem that he had fashioned out of clay. In Jewish folklore, a golem is an animated being, created entirely from inanimate matter. Adam, as described in the Talmud, was created as a golem when his dust was "kneaded into a shapeless hunk." This is an apt metaphor for the Jewish people as perceived by Hitler and his henchmen, in particular the likes of an Albert Eichmann; to him, Jews were no more than "shapeless hunks!"

Though in more than one instance, Eichmann was willing to trade these "shapeless hunks" for trucks and miscellaneous goods; eventually he settled upon money.

I first learned of this episode from Robert St. John, once the "golden voice" of NBC, a journalist, lecturer, and author of some twenty-two books. My wife and I were close friends with Robert and his wife, Ruth. Eventually, I became St. John's biographer, writing *Merchant of Words*.

As all of Europe was crumbled about them, the largest Jewish remnant was in Hungary. As long as its 800,000 Jews remained, Hitler and his henchman Adolf Eichmann could never say Europe was *Judenrein* (cleansed of Jews).

In 1944, deportations, mostly to Auschwitz reached a furious pace. Against this backdrop, Rudolph Kasztner, a Hungarian Jew, along with Joel Brand and a small Jewish committee headquartered in Budapest—*Va'ada Egra we Hazalah* or the Council for Assistance and Rescue, *Va'ada* for short, set out to save the lives of as many Hungarian Jews as possible. Kasztner, a wheeler-dealer of sorts, devised a scheme to bribe the Nazis.

Kasztner (and his group) reached the ears of Adolf Eichmann who, at first, said he wanted "none of your little deals." Then he suggested if *Va'ada* really wanted to cut a deal, he, Eichmann, would turn over to the committee one million Jews in exchange for ten thousand fully equipped trucks that the Wehrmacht desperately needed.

The suggestion was absurd, even Eichmann's promise that the trucks would be used to fight the Russians. Nonetheless, the parties were at least talking.

Brand was sent to Turkey in a futile attempt to begin discussions with the Americans and British. He was arrested.

Back in Budapest, a mini-version of the proposal was agreed upon—1,676 Jewish men, women, and children in return for Kasztner's collected treasure (mostly in jewelry, gold and banknotes). The chosen would board a specially chartered train that would allow them to debark in neutral Switzerland, or some other country—perhaps Spain.

The manner of how to select 1,676 Jews out of a nation of 800,000 was one of the major ingredients of the transaction that drew Robert St. John to the story. He called it a "perfect example of the agony of war." It mixed morality with ethics with politics with pragmatism with compassion. After first selecting those who had given him (Kasztner) their money, their wives and children, Kasztner's wife and close relatives—who then?

Kasztner's story continued in Israel in the 1950s when Kasztner, by then a official in Ben Gurion's Mapai party, was accused in a pamphlet of being a collaborator with the Nazis. He sued for defamation, lost the case, and while waiting for his appeal to be decided, was assassinated in March 1957. (The decision was overturned the next year in his favor).

St. John had long wanted to write about "people faced with the necessity of making excruciating life and death decisions in time of war." He gave a proposal to Doubleday and reach an agreement with them to write a book. It was suggested by his editor that he tell the story as fiction so although in almost all respects the narrative is accurate, the names have been changed. In the book, Rezső Kasztner becomes Andor Horvath.

In 1962, *The Man Who Played God: A Novel of Hungary and Israel, 1944-1956* was published. It was a Literary Guild selection and widely-read in multiple editions.

While at an annual Beethoven birthday party, I first met the major subject of this book, Manny Mandel. We struck up a conversation, and soon a friendship blossomed between Manny, his wife, Adrienne, and the Horowitzes.

During one of our many subsequent tête-à-têtes, I learned that Manny, then known as Imi, at age eight, along with his mother and an uncle were three of the Jewish men, women, and children aboard Kasztner's train! His father, a famous cantor, was not with them; he had been working in a Nazi run forced labor camp *(Munkatabor)* in the Ukraine, where the Germans were fighting the Russians, though during the time of this episode, he had snuck off in the night and made his way back to Budapest.

Knowing of the story as St. John told it, I was intrigued. Later, I came to understand that Manny's journey, from Budapest to the Bergen-Belsen Concentration camp, and then to Switzerland,

Israel and finally to the United States shows us not only the per-
severance of the Mandel family through times of trouble and
tragedy and change, but also give us insights into Jewish life in
Hungary and the community's fate during the Holocaust.

In more recent years, Manny Mandel has lectured tireless-
ly both at the United States Holocaust Memorial Museum and
at events around the world. He not only tells his own story but
gives voice to those who can no longer speak from themselves.

He has been most generous with his time, helping me draw
a more accurate picture of him and his family. In addition , I was
given access to four lengthy tapes of testimony of Manny and
his father, two from the Holocaust Museum, and two from the
Shoah Foundation.

With the facts brought together here, we will now have
a more complete picture of the history and lives of the family
Mandel.

One

Five-year-old Imi Mandel heard loud rapping on the front door of his Aunt Magda's apartment in Novi Sad, a thriving municipality in what was once the Yugoslavian kingdom of Serbia.

Roused from a restless sleep, Imi sat up in the early dawn light in time to see his father, Lajos, open the bedroom door where he and Ella had been sleeping. Lajos left it ajar, hastening to intercept Magda just as she was about to unlock the front door.

Smiling, she waved him off. "It's only the maid, Lajos."

For an instant Imi felt a gust of the brutally cold January wind. The maid and Magda spoke in whispers but Imi thought he heard Magda, turning to Lajos, repeat "There's a razzia (raid) going on outside! They're gathering Jews in the street!"

Imi had heard that word before—*razzia*—but he wasn't sure what it meant, though, from their expressions, he suspected it had to be something horrendous. Ella came up behind Imi and placed her hands reassuringly on his shoulders.

It had been nearly a year since the Axis Powers, led by

Germany, had invaded and partitioned the territory. It was annexed by Hungary.

Tying her bathrobe about her slender body, *Magda-Neni* (Aunt Magda) approached Imi and Ella. Imi marveled at how similar in stature and facial features she was to *Anyu* (Mother). Both sisters were slender and gangly; Ella was an inch taller than her husband Lajos. Imi thought the sisters were quite beautiful, with silky brunette hair that cascaded down their backs, nearly reaching their shoulder blades.

Imi, an only child, was sure that he was *Magda-Neni's* "very favorite person in the whole wide world." After all, it was she, while visiting Budapest, who first recognized that he was coming down with a cold, and she who had suggested to Ella that the whole family travel south to Novi Sad to visit with her and Ella's parents, Imi's grandparents, Armin and Paula Klein. They would stay with Magda in her apartment. Lajos was able to find a colleague to take over his *Fokantor's* duties for a few days, allowing him to join them for a short three or four day vacation.

While Lajos and Ella were huddled together, whispering, Magda pressed her hand on her nephew's forehead. "Imi, you've still got a fever." She looked down at his tiny feet. "And you're barefooted. You know better than that; you'll catch your death of cold."

Ella and Lajos were no longer whispering; they were talking animatedly and gesticulating with their hands. Lajos knit his brow, "some Jews must have been caught fighting with the partisans! This is probably their retribution!" Then he muttered to himself, "Lord knows, we've done our best to assimilate, but at the same time we've tried not to lose our Jewishness. No little task."

After shaking his head, he hunched up his powerful shoulders and raised his palms upwards, while wedging in his favorite word: "Who has the *cognizance* of how the Gentile mind works? I certainly don't."

"What's happening?" Imi asked, tugging at Magda's sleeve. "What did the maid say?"

"Let's wait and let your father explain it to you, Imi." She turned, saying to herself, *Thank God Sanyi isn't here.*

"Does it have something to do with our being Jewish?"

Magda nodded just as Imi sneezed three times in rapid succession.

"*Gesundheit, Gesundheit, Gesundheit!* Now get off of your feet and come back to bed."

Imi was fully awake. "I'm not sleepy anymore. Where is Uncle Sanyi?"

"He's away somewhere." She closed her eyes, and sighed. When she opened them, she smiled, looking down at her nephew. "How would you like it if I read some more to you? What would you rather hear, Robinson Crusoe Kalandjai [*The Adventures of Robinson Crusoe*] or Tamas Batya Kunyhoja [*Uncle Tom's Cabin*]?"

"Robinson Crusoe,

"But," Imi knit his broad, high brow, "Aunt Magda, please tell me, why is he always crying?"

"Why is who always crying? What do *you mean*, Imi?"

Imi reached for the book, and, thumbing through it, pointed to the word, "sir," which in Hungarian meant "cry." Magda smiled, before explaining that Friday addressed Robinson Crusoe as "Sir." She tousled her nephew's thick, dirty-blond hair, no longer curly. Imi shrugged his teeny shoulders. All of a sudden he thought of his pet parakeet, which he kept in the apartment in Pest. He hoped Margit, their maid, had remembered to feed it while they were gone.

There was another, more insistent, knock at the front door. "I'll get it," said Lajos. He opened the door, and found himself facing an unsmiling *Csendor* (noise policeman). He pushed past Lajos and shouted loudly, "Everyone hurry, get dressed, and then come with me!" He glanced at the grandfather's clock near the door. It was exactly two minutes to twelve. He looked at his watch and realized the clock was broken. Frowning, he looked up and said, "Wear something warm. We have to take a census."

Uniformed armed Hungarian *Nyilas* (fascist Arrow Cross Party), both policemen and soldiers, surrounded the long column, four rows wide, of frightened Jews and Serbs. At first, Imi, shivering, held onto both his father and mother's hands as they, Magda-Neni, and many other Jews quick-stepped along the slippery cobblestone streets. Occasionally they made eye contact with one of the seemingly nonplussed gentile pedestrians. Hungarians had expelled Jews before. Besides, war was war.

Before long, the stocky and muscular Lajos wrapped his fur coat around Imi and scooped him up into his arms. Imi, who was still feverish, felt his father's burly arms pressing him close to his barrel chest, as they made their way toward the Danube River. He could barely hear *Apa* (father) reciting Psalms softly to himself.

> *I am not afraid of ten thousands of people,*
> *That have set themselves against me round about..."*

Imi closed his eyes, embracing the cadence of his father's voice.

> *All my enemies shall be ashamed and sore affrighted;*
> *They shall turn back, they shall be ashamed suddenly.*

Imi looked at his mother; she and Magda were crying. He mouthed the words: "I love you, Anyu. I love you Magda-Neni."

> *Behold mine affliction at the hands of them that hate me;*
> *Thou that liftest me up from the gates of death;...*

Imi looked up at his father's round face; his head was bowed, his body davening.

> *My God, my God, why has Thou forsaken me,*
> *And art far from my help at the words of my cry?*

When *Apa* began the twenty-third Psalm, Imi recited with him:

> *...Yea, though I walk through the valley of the shadow of death,*

I will fear no evil,
For Thou art with me;
Thy rod and Thy staff, they comfort me...

Lajos kissed the top of Imi's head. Imi was sure *Apa* was speaking directly to him when he said:

God is our refuge and strength, A very present help in trouble.

They were rapidly approaching the Danube.

Deliver me out of the mire, and let me not sink;
Let me be delivered from them that hate me, and out of the deep waters.

Imi recognized the words from the hundredth Psalm:

Enter into His gates with thanksgiving,
And into His courts with praise;
Give thanks unto Him, and bless His name.
For the Lord is good; His mercy endureth for ever;
And His faithfulness unto all generations...

Peering up at his father's normally jovial, but now so sad face, Imi said, "Apa, where are Nagyanya [Grandmother] and Nagyapa [Grandfather]?"

"They're coming by truck, Imi."

Soon Lajos could hear what he surmised to be the sound of shooting—"Ta, ta, ta, ta!" Several people in front of them were crying; some threw themselves on the hard snow-frozen ground, others attempted to run away, but were forced back at gunpoint. One elderly man was hit on the head by the metal barrel part of a rifle; he crawled back on his hands and knees, bleeding profusely, leaving blood-spattered stains in the snow.

Lajos was still carrying Imi as they approached the high stockade fence surrounding the large public *strand* (beach); because of the flat terrain, it blocked much of their view of the normally brownish Danube River, which was now a glistening white, frozen solid several inches thick. The temperature had dropped throughout the night to minus ten degrees Celsius. Every now and then their captors fired cannons onto the ice, probing it open.

Far ahead of them, beyond an open, duel-hinged wooden entry gate, Lajos could barely make out men, women and children being driven onto the ice, where they were shot in the back.

As if to justify his actions, one insipid Hungarian gendarme shouted: "Everyone who's here is an enemy of Hungary!" Faces contorted with terror and agony, they were shoved by the butt-end of rifles and machine guns to a special location, where they were unceremoniously shot. Their limp bodies were tossed, like flour sacks, into the icy waters of the left bank of the Danube. Blood erupted to the surface in bubbly red patches, as their bodies disappeared beneath the icy water. Hours before the Sabbath began, the bathing spot had become the killing spot.

For what seemed like hours, they inched their way forward. The roofs of the barracks-like Petrovaradin Fortress came into view. Covered with snow, it was like a fairyland, like a still life of a Walt Disney cartoon – perhaps a frozen moment out of *Snow White and the Seven Dwarfs* or a monochromatic panorama from *Fantasia*.

A voice rang out in Hungarian. "Fokantor, Ur! [Chief Cantor, Sir] What are you doing here? You're not a Chetnik. [one of the Serbian resistance groups]."

Lajos wheeled around. He immediately recognized the policeman, who often worked as a traffic cop for crowd control in the narrow street in front of the Rumbach Synagogue whenever they had services.

Pointing to Lajos, the policeman yelled, "Stand aside!" For a moment, Lajos wasn't sure how to respond. What kind of reaction might the other guards have? Finally Lajos shouted, "We were visiting our family." A long private conversation ensued.

While they were still talking, a German lieutenant in a staff car drove up. Highly excited, the policeman addressed the lieutenant. Pointing toward Lajos, he said, "That man is the Chief Cantor from the Rumbach Synagogue in Pest."

The lieutenant shrugged. "Take them all inside the gymnasium." Showing little emotion, he added, "I've just gotten a cabled order that the killings have been called off. Take all of this vermin there!"

The survivors were marched back to a nearby school.

Inside the gymnasium, Lajos, Imi, Ella and Magda met up with *Nagyanya* and *Nagyapa*, Armin and Paula Klein. For nearly two hours, they sat together on the floor. At last, everyone was told to go home.

The sun had gone down. After seeing Armin and Paula leave, Lajos hailed a cab, which took him, Ella, Imi and Magda back to her apartment. As soon as they returned, Magda phoned her sister, Ilona. Until recently, Ilona had lived with her husband, Erno Krishaber, in nearby Ruma, where they owned a small tannery factory but it had a short time ago been taken over by the Nazis. They had moved back to Novi Sad before Erno was sent to a labor camp.

"You won't believe this," said Ilona. "A policeman knocked on my door. I invited him in and served him coffee and cake, which he enjoyed. And then he left. Thank God, I didn't have to go to the beach."

The following morning was the Sabbath. Lajos was sure God would understand. The family gathered their things, then Lajos flagged down a one-horse sleigh, a winter taxi, which took them to the train station where they boarded a lumbering, smoke filled, but comfortable rail car. Soon they would be back in the safety of home.

After stopping at a number of stations along the way, they arrived 160 miles north in Budapest.

They never returned to Novi Sad, the "quaint village," which had completely lost its innocence. This time, Lajos and Ella left Novi Sad for good, hoping to put the day's traumatic, near-death experience behind them and their only son, Imi.

On that tragic day, 550 Jews and 292 Serbs were driven on to the ice of the Danube and killed, literally, in *cold* blood. After disappearing in the Danube, their corpses were carried all the way to Belgrade and beyond where they continued to be spotted for weeks.

During this incident, Magda's in-laws, the Hajdus, had been shot and killed near their own house a few miles away. More than likely, after a curfew in which phone and telegraph lines were severed street by street, bringing complete isolation to the area, they were killed outside while their apartment was searched and plundered. The pretext, if one was even needed, was probably a charge of "collaborating with the partisans."

Subsequent accounts vary. One reported that during three days between January 21st and 23rd, 1942, Hungarian policemen, many under the influence of rum, had killed a total of 1,246 citizens; among them were more than 800 Jews. Another reported that 550 Jews and 292 Serbs were driven into the ice. Still another had the total death toll of the Novi Sad *razzia*, organized by the local army commander, a senior Hungarian officer, at around 2,500. A later, "official count" lists a total of 4,116, which included 2,842 Serbs, 1,250 Jews, 11 Hungarians, and 13 Russians. Whatever the actual number, it was an atrocious episode; the massacre only stopped when Novi Sad's governor, Leo Deak, got through to his superiors.

Two

Toward the end of the eighteenth century, Holy Roman Emperor Joseph II of Austria, considered to be an enlightened despot, introduced a Patent (or Edict) of Tolerance that granted certain new freedoms to non-Roman Catholic Christians. Later, it was extended to Jews."

He also issued a decree to the effect that every Jew should adopt a German surname. Heretofore, Jews had been referred to as, say, Emanuel, the son of Yehudah, or Gabriella, the daughter of Armin.

Thus, it is not surprising that so many of today's Jews, with roots in Europe, have great difficulty in tracing their family tree beyond the *fin-de-siecle*. This is certainly true for the family Mandel, whose early roots are shrouded in obscurity. The surname could have its origins in the German and Yiddish name for almond or refer to a place or even be a variant of the Yiddish first name, Mendel.

Manny Mandel has no idea when his family first came to Hungary or its neighboring municipalities, nor does he know what his ancestors did or accomplished during their unrecorded existence.

It is recorded that some Jews from Belgrade appeared to have settled in Novi Sad (*Ujvidek* in Hungarian, *Neusatz* in German) at the foot of the later Petrovardin Fortress in the sixteenth century. However, most Hungarian Jews came from Nikolsburg in Moravia.

By and large, Jews supported the 1848 revolution in Hungary for which they subsequently received full citizenship. Yet, in 1875, in Parliament, there were demands for the expulsion of Jews from Hungary. Six years later, Zionist pioneers began the first *aliyah* (ascension—immigration into Palestine). These Hungarian Zionists sought to liberate Jews from the yoke of the diaspora. Jews numbered approximately six percent of the population, but in Jerusalem, they nearly constituted a majority.

We know that Lajos's father, Avraham Mandel, was born in 1877, in Csepe, Hungary (later Czechoslovakia, now in the Ukraine), a small Ruthenaian-Hungarian village. He attended a *Yeshiva* (institute of higher learning), but was never employed as a rabbi. He inherited land and/or funds from his father-in-law and had a farm of sorts—raised grain and other crops. Later, he courted bankruptcy, encouraging his daughter, Helen, to travel to America where a cousin lived, so the family would have one less mouth to feed. He could read and write Hungarian and worked as a regional registrar. He died in 1930 at the age of fifty-three—the same year that Lajos and Ella were married. Avraham's wife, Rosa Braun (Mandel), was born in 1878 or 1879. She wore a *shaytl* (traditional woman's wig). Manny's father added, "She baked, washed, and raised her seven children: Lajos, Jeno, Bela, Dezso, Helen, Rivka, and Esther; she lost three others." Imi was given permission to call Rosa by her family sobriquet, "Mama. "

Lajos, like his father, was born in the small village of Csepe on March 3, 1904 and given the name Yehudah Leib Mandel. That became "Lajos" in Hungarian. At the time of his birth, in Budapest, the capital of Hungary, "The City of Baths," Jews made up a quarter of the population. More than half of the physicians, and nearly half of the lawyers and journalists were Jewish. Jews were also prominent in government service, and in the municipal administrations. For better or worse, most of these Jews supported the Magyars, the dominant ethnic group in Hungary.

Between 1905 and 1914, a second wave of Jews made *aliyah* to Palestine. Theodor Herzl, the father of political Zionism, was born and raised in Budapest. They were true believers, motivated by the aborted Russian Revolution of 1905 and bloody pogroms throughout the Pale of Settlement.

Avraham and Rosa and their children were extremely religious, as were most of the Jewish inhabitants of Csepe. All of the boys attended the local *Cheder* (Jewish elementary school) and later, the *Yeshiva*, where students study the *Talmud*—the collection of ancient rabbinic writings consisting of the *Mishnah* and the *Gemara*, the basis of religious authority in Orthodox Judaism. On the other hand, Jewish girls were brought up to get married, get pregnant, and raise large families. Education was secondary—Blu Greenberg in her charming book, *How to Run a Traditional Jewish Household* speaks of the three *mitzvot* (blessings) accorded women: (1) *challah* (removing a token amount of dough—the size of an olive—from a yeast batter, and throwing it into the oven fires while reciting the proper blessing); (2) *nerot* (candle lighting); and (3) *Niddah* (women) during menstruation in a state of sexual unavailability. Although Greenberg represents a somewhat more modern approach to orthodox Judaism, her descriptions would not be out of place in most orthodox Jewish households of the early twentieth century.

Ruthenia had two churches, a Catholic and a Reformed.

The priest at the Catholic Church espoused a common prejudice about Jews. During Passover, he was heard to say, "The Jews are looking for blood [of] the matzoh!" He also emphasized the Jews role in the killing of Christ. Spurred on by these canards, the Catholic children had no qualms about beating Lajos and his friends with heavy sticks. Fortunately, the priest from the Reformed Church was more conciliatory toward the Jews.

Starting at the age of three, Lajos went to *Cheder* in Nagyszolos and Munkach. By the age of four, he was able to read Hebrew. *Cheder* was all consuming—it began at 6:00 AM with morning services. At 8:00 AM, he left to go to public school where he remained until noon, when he returned to *Cheder*. He had lunch, and went back to the regular public school and returned to *Cheder* from 4:00–6:30 PM.

At the age of eight, Lajos realized he had a nice voice. He even performed on the festival days. Between the ages of twelve and fourteen, he was in Nagyszolos where he was not allowed to go to the regular public school though he was permitted to take an examination at the end of the year. In 1917, he celebrated his bar mitzvah.

In his question-and-answer testimony for the United States Holocaust Museum, Lajos, by then referred to as Yehudah, commented: "My upbringing was so strict that we wouldn't walk past a Reformed Temple [Christian Church]—we passed to the other side of the street. The discipline was immense; everyone stuck to the rules of the Yeshiva. "

Imi's mother, Gabriella, known all her life as Ella, was born in Kunszentmiklos, Hungary on January 20, 1908. She was raised in what was then, a small town, Novi Sad ("new planting" in Serbian), Yugoslavia; it was ethnically Hungarian. She spoke Serbo-Croatian because the end of the First World War saw the dissolution of the Austro-Hungarian Empire.

In her youth it was a city of 3,000 Jews, and one synagogue.

Her father, Armin Klein, was the rabbi of the congregation. He spoke Hungarian, Yiddish and German but not Serbo-Croatian. Because of his inability, or perhaps his unwillingness, to speak this language, he resigned his role as rabbi and became the chief administrator of the Jewish community. He and his wife, Paula raised six children, three girls, and three boys—Magda, Ilona, Ella, Sanyi, Jeno and Zsiga.

During World War I, Austro-Hungarian Jews numbered more than two and a half million. They were quite loyal to the Magyar fatherland. Approximately three hundred thousand Jews served in the armed forces, many of them high-ranking officers, and even some generals. A number were decorated for valor. Over ten thousand Jews died in the conflict; many thousands were wounded and disabled. Still, the majority of Jewish boys and young men continued to remain in their villages, and study at a *Cheder* or Yeshiva. However due to the "nationalistic movement" the "improved Cheders" were established, where studies began to be conducted in Hebrew, and where secular subjects were also taught.

After Russia aligned herself with the entente powers of Britain and France, Jews hoped that this might herald a change in Russia's traditional anti-Jewish policy. This was not to be the case. Many Jews were expelled from the front lines, seized as hostages and, on occasion, attacked in pogroms. When the Cossacks crossed the borders into Bukovina and Galicia, thousands of Jewish subjects of Austro-Hungary became fugitives, fleeing westward.

After the post-war Treaty of Trianon, Czechoslovakia was born. Austria became a much diminished state, and Hungary, now having shrunk to a fraction of its prewar self—losing half of its population—was now shorn of Transylvania and Slovakia, two independent regions. In Hungary, though Jews had maintained a heroic role in the war and a "creative role in the peace," the "Awakening Magyars," through myriad "clauses" began to restrict Jewish students in high schools and universities. Still, Jews felt liberated, unafraid to lead their own private lives, confident that they could continue to forge a restrictive (sans Gentiles) Jewish life in their own ghetto-like enclaves. After the signing of the cease-fire agreements, one manifestation of this independent Jewish political movement was the establishment of *nationalraten* (national councils).

In 1918, when Lajos was fourteen, his father, Avraham, spoke with the local rabbi and asked that his son be allowed to sing in the choir. This privilege was denied. However, Cantor Gottleib, a friend of Avraham, realized that Lajos indeed had a nice voice; he wanted him to join the choir. This pleased Lajos, who was not lacking in self-confidence, but the rabbi had other ideas. He encouraged Avraham to send Lajos to the *Nagyszolos Yeshiva* in a small town, fifteen kilometers away, north of the corner where Hungary, Slovakia, and the Ukraine borders meet.

Two years later, Avraham asked if Lajos's younger brother, six-year-old Dezso, who still dressed as a little boy, could study, too. The rabbi lowered his head, looking over his spectacles, he said, "No, I don't have a Cheder here; I have a big Yeshiva."

Straightening up to his full, yet slight, posture, Avraham replied, "But, Dezso knows the Talmud; he can recite forty pages by heart." The rabbi appeared skeptical, but agreed to test the boy. Dezso performed to perfection.

The rabbi, pulling on his beard, said, "Your fourth boy, Dezso, buy him long pants and he can study here."

In 1919, numerous Jewish organizations petitioned the League of Nations with regard to treatment of the Jews, drawing attention to treaty violations in Poland and Hungary. However, both nations insisted that this constituted intervention in "foreign factors," an intrusion into their internal affairs. The Joint Foreign Committee and the *Alliance Israelite* submitted a petition concerning "numerous clauses" in Hungarian universities. Out of fear that this would inevitably lead to a worsening of the universities authority toward them, representatives of the Jewish community in Hungary protested.

That same year, there was a Communist revolt in Hungary (March-August, 1919). Bela Kun, a Jew, led the attempted revolution. Several other Jews held important positions in his fledgling government. The following year, using military force, Admiral Miklos Horthy succeeded in taking over the reins of government. He launched a series of anti-Semitic *razzias*, which became known as The White Terror. Many Jews were tortured or killed; the bodies of the victims were tossed into the Danube.

As an aftermath, Hungary established a quota system for universities. Their justification? Sixty percent of the Hungarian doctors, fifty percent of the lawyers, and forty percent of all musicians in Hungary were Jewish. Eighty-eight percent of members of the stock exchange, and ninety-one percent of the currency brokers were Jewish. Instituting a rather bizarre "affirmative action" policy, the "numerous clauses" law, writ large, concerning admission to the universities now gave priority to the Magyar students, from what were formerly Hungarian provinces, rather than to Jewish students.

While at the Yeshiva in Ungvar, Lajos was able to lead most any religious service. For four years, he studied there before receiving a *Smicha* (ordination—a written document indicating that he qualified as a rabbi).

The *Chazzan* asked Lajos to sing in the choir during the High Holy Days. Once someone heard him singing and asked, "Who's the Chazzan?"

The reply was,"He's not a Chazzan, he's just one of us in the choir."

Nevertheless, Lajos was asked if he would perform services for the congregation. He performed and got paid for it. This went on from month to month. Smiling to himself, in a 1989 interview, he reflected that, "I became a star. I maintained myself."

After commencement, at age eighteen, Lajos was drafted into the Czech army, where he, a seminarian, served as a non-combatant corpsman. The most frequent service he provided was administering sulfur powder to wounds caused by vehicular accidents and sometimes by animals that gored.

In November, the birthday of the president of Czechoslovakia occured. To celebrate it, a lieutenant, known as the "Superintendent of Entertainment," asked if anyone had a nice voice; he needed someone to sing in Smetana's comic opera, *The Bartered Bride*.

Some of Lajos's friends told the lieutenant that Lajos had a very nice voice but knew nothing about opera. The lieutenant asked him if he was willing to learn. Lajos hesitated, before being ordered to report to the lieutenant's office. When he arrived, Lajos auditioned by singing a Hungarian song. The lieutenant liked it. Phrase by phrase, note by note, the first lieutenant taught Lajos to sing *The Bartered Bride* in Czech.

> Hear the soaring skylark singing.
> Joy and sunshine far and near; far and near,
> Now that lovely spring is here; spring is here.
> Now that lovely spring is here; spring is here.
> Though young hearts are quickly captured
> In this fair and sunny season –
> Though young hearts are quickly captured in this fair and
> sunny season, Do not give your word forever
> Til you look on love with reason.

The officer assured Lajos that he would push him forward whenever he had to go on or tell him when to get off the stage.

The show went on, and even though Lajos couldn't read a note of music, the regimental commander was impressed with Lajos's voice as the tenor lead.

During Lajos's tenure in the army, "patriotic" gangs roamed the streets, wreaking vengeance on the Jews for their alleged role in the failed Communist revolution during the spring and summer of 1919. It was now 1923. Two years later brought an upsurge of nationalistic feeling among the majority of people in the new states. They had won their political independence, and this nationalistic awakening caused great anxiety in the various minority groups, most particularly the Jews. Any and all appeals succeeded in escalating the hostility and bullying in Poland, Romania and Hungary. *Razzias* broke out all over Eastern Europe.

In April of 1924, Lajos was scheduled to be discharged from the army. The regimental commander said to him: "You don't know any music. You have a beautiful voice. I'll apply to the appropriate division and try to get you a scholarship at the Prague Academy so you can pursue an operatic career."

Wary of asking his father for permission to make this career move, Lajos called on his mother's brother, Moses Braun Bolgar, a respected attorney. Would Moses visit with his father to broach the subject?

Avraham's response: "Mozsi, I have four sons and three daughters. If Lajos becomes a singer for the goyim, and desecrates the holidays, I will have six children."

Much later, Yehuda summed it up: "It wasn't the way a Jew should lead his life. It was the end of my [operatic] career."

"Better you should get married," said Lajos's father. Lajos knew what that meant—an arranged marriage. "The bride-to-be's father has a general store. You'll be the cashier and study all day until you become a Talmud Chacham [educated Jew]."

"I didn't want to wed. I wanted to study music." There was

to be no music academy, and no marriage. Lajos said, "I'm going back to the Yeshiva."

After the army, Lajos moved to Pozsony (German Pressburg), also known as, Bratislava, the capital of the Slovak Republic. The tiny village was on the Danube, near the meeting point of Slovakia, Austria and Hungary, at the foot of the Little Carpathian mountain range. It was a city with nearly eleven thousand Jews, a Great Synagogue, and many smaller ones, referred to as prayer houses, mostly Orthodox. Most of its Jews maintained an affinity toward Germany; however, the educated class was more empathetic toward Hungary. The Hungarian community was split almost everywhere into Orthodox and Neolog, a relatively new doctrine (circa 1868—whereby Jews may contribute fully to society without compromising Torah principles in their lives). The divided communities were united only by their trend into national associations which, in many ways, constituted a cohesive force in Jewish life. Lajos studied with the Neologists at the Yeshiva.

For over a year, unbeknown to his father, while at the Yeshiva, Lajos had been traveling periodically to Vienna, where he had a singing teacher. Part of his training was to lie on his back with heavy books piled upon his diaphragm.

Also, without his father's knowledge, Lajos had been spending weekends in small communities where he *davened* Friday night and Saturday at their synagogues. The income offset his costs and allowed him to send some money home where it was welcomed. As the eldest son, he felt responsible for sending funds home to where his younger brothers, Eugene, Jeno and Dezso, were still in school. At one of these communities, a man approached him and asked about his possible interest in the Cantor's *Hochschule*, the world renowned Cantor's Institute in Vienna run by Cantors Fischer, Margolius and Muller. Lajos immediately realized this would be the opportunity to study music and learn more of his craft. He was closely examined at the Institute and accepted.

After about three years of study in Vienna, Lajos received a diploma that stated in German that he had completed his program. The words on the diploma were "frequentierte und absolvierte."

Soon, the newly minted and highly qualified cantor was offered the pulpit at the Seitenstettengasse, "Sulzer's" Temple, the prestigious synagogue in Vienna where the legendary Cantor Salomon Sulzer had served. Sulzer was author of the magnum opus, *Schir Zion*; composed of transcriptions and arrangements of ancient traditional Jewish melodies.

This was quite an honor. Nevertheless, while in Vienna, Lajos was motivated to audition in Novi Sad. Before long, he was notified by phone that he had been selected.

As Yehuda later described: "The Novi Sad synagogue was a magnificent place, with eight-hundred families, an organ, an organist, and a mixed choir of men and women."

He took the position as *fokantor* there because it was ethnically Hungarian, and he felt his having served in this location would enhance his prospects for a post in the Hungarian capital, Budapest, the quintessential pulpit, the pot of gold at the end of the cantorial rainbow.

Three

While serving as the *Fokantor* in Novi Sad's synagogue, Lajos met Gabriella Klein, daughter of the Jewish Community Administrator and former Rabbi. He courted; she responded. They were married in 1930. Neither was overly demonstrative, but they appeared to have a solid relationship, based on mutual respect. The following year, Lajos's father, Avraham, died. In 1933, Lajos and Ella's first born child, a boy, Reuven, developed an absorption problem, which in those days was untreatable. At ten weeks old, he died of starvation and was buried in Novi Sad.

For the benefit of the Yeshivas, Lajos had sung two services in Kovno (Kaunas), the capital of Lithuania, a center of Jewish learning. A man named Hershkovitch from Kovno was in attendance, liked what he heard, and asked Lajos if he wished to further his musical career. He suggested that Lajos could study music in Mr. Hershkovitch's mansion.

Lajos jumped at the opportunity, and was provided with a horse and carriage that would take him wherever he wanted to

Wedding of Ella and Lajos Mandel, Novisad, June 1930.

go while studying in Kovno. At the same time, he also traveled to Belgrade, where he gave concerts over the state radio. During that period, he was invited for *probes* in Groningen, and Hoek, both in Holland and London. He was selected by the Dukes Place Synagogue, also known as "The Great Synagogue," in London, which was later destroyed during a German air raid in May, 1942. He declined the offer, still hoping for an opportunity in Budapest.

He had a "Verdi" tenor voice, a veritable *lyrico spinto*; able to be pushed to be big, and booming. He had a range of two and a half octaves, and could hit a brilliant high C. When pressed, could reach a "D."

As Lajos traveled to European cities from his position in Novi Sad, he developed a growing reputation but his interest in a position in Budapest remained; it was thwarted by the authorities. As a Jew and a Czech citizen he had been drafted into the Czech Army. Czech citizens were denied working papers in Hungary.

The city of Riga in Latvia also had a major Jewish community and its Cantor of forty years, the revered Baruch Leib Rosovsky, had retired in the late 1920s. As usual in such congregations, *probes* were held. Lajos applied. He was among the final candidates with Hermann Jadlowker, a native of Riga, who had just returned from serving as a leading tenor at the Metropolitan Opera in New York. A third applicant was a well reputed Cantor, Israel Alter from Hannover, Germany. Alter went on to a significant career in South Africa.

While in Riga auditioning, Lajos met and formed a relationship with the Rogochover Rov who was there for treatment of a serious medical condition. That "Rebbe," Joseph Rozin, (1858-1936) was impressed with the 29 year old Cantor who had an excellent Jewish education and a magnificent voice. He wrote to the Riga congregation and suggested that Mandel be their choice because he was "not only a fine cantor but a Talmid Chochem." In 1933, Lajos was selected for the Riga position.

Lajos was escorted around Riga by a prominent member of the Jewish community. A highly cultured city made up primarily of Latvians and Russians, Riga was also home to over forty thousand Jews, many crowded into Maskavas, a heavily populated Jewish neighborhood just southeast of Old Town. Situated on the Baltic Sea, the Latvian city was famous for its Art Nouveau (*Jugendstil*) architecture.

It had an opera house, many synagogues, and a Yeshiva. The the main synagogue of the city, *Grosse Chor Shule* was burned to the ground in July 1941 with the congregants trapped inside. At the same time the old Jewish cemetery became a killing ground.

In the decade between 1925 and 1935, at least six thousand Jews, many of them Zionists, had left Latvia, the majority made *aliyah* — immigration to Palestine.

Lajos had been offered a lifetime contract to remain *forkantor* in Novi Sad, but decided to take the position as *oberkantor* (German for Chief Cantor) in Riga. His ultimate aim remained a position in Budapest. Why Riga? Rozofsky had stepped down after serving there as *oberkantor* for forty years. To succeed him would be commensurate with being the successor to Toscanini, or following in the footsteps of *Oberkantor* Zulzer in Vienna. Lajos was building up quite an impressive curriculum vitae, having already received a *Smicha* (ordination) from two seminaries, training in Vienna, and serving as *oberkantor* at his second major synagogue.

In January of 1933, Hitler came to power in Germany. Within a few months, a boycott of Jewish businesses had begun. Yellow Stars of David and anti-Jewish slogans were painted on windows and buildings throughout the country

There was a long, squalid history of such vindictive actions that singled out the Jewish community. As early as the year 807, Abbassid Caliph Haroun al-Raschid ordered all Jews to wear a yellow belt and a tall cone-like hat. Such symbolism reached its heyday during the thirteenth century. In 1215, Pope Innocent III issued his famous four decrees covering Jews. Among them was a requirement that Jews wear a distinguishing badge and "characteristic" clothing. Two years later, King Henry III of England ordered Jews to wear, "on the front of their upper garment, the two tablets of the Ten Commandments made of white linen or parchment."

In 1267, the Council of Vienna decreed that all Jews were to wear horned hats (*pileum cornutum*) to demonstrate that they were progeny of the devil. Amongst the populace, fairy tales abounded: it was thought that the hat would cover up the real horns growing out of Jewish heads (one is reminded of Michelangelo's famous sculpture of a horned Moses created three-centuries later). In France, which heretofore had had many variations of the badge, Louis IX decreed in 1269 that "both men and women were to wear badges on the outer garment, both front and back, round pieces of yellow felt or linen, a palm long and four fingers wide."

A decade later, in 1279, at the Synod of Buda held during the reign of King Ladislaus IV, it was decreed in the presence of the papal ambassador, "that every Jew appearing in public should wear, on the left side of his upper garment, a piece of red cloth." In the later half of the thirteenth century, Jews of Germany and Austria were distinguished by being forced to wear a "horned hat," other- wise known as a "Jewish hat." This was an article of clothing that some debonair Jews had worn freely before the crusades; now it had become mandatory.

During the fifteenth century, a badge became the distinguishing article for the Jews of Germany and Austria. In 1434, the Jews of Augsburg were required to wear a yellow wheel on their clothng. In 1457, Archbishop Diether of Mayence required the Jews of Frankfort to wear distinctive markings on their clothing. Between 1780 and 1790, Joseph II, the successor of Maria Theresa issued a decree known as the *Systematica Gentis Judaicae* (regulations for Jews) which, in one stroke, wiped out the previous decrees that had oppressed Jews for centuries. Amongst these decrees was one that abolished all distinctive marks "hitherto" worn by Jews; they might even carry swords. However, they were required to discard their distinctive marks prescribed by their religion, and to shave their beards. To this, the Orthodox community objected.

Two years after taking over the reins of power in Germany, Hitler said: "If international finance—Jewry inside and outside Europe—should succeed in throwing the nation into another world war, the result will be the Bolshevization of the earth and thus a victory of Jewry, but the destruction of the Jewish race in Europe!" He would come dangerously close to fulfilling the last part of this prophecy.

On May 8, 1936, in Riga, Ella gave birth to a second son; his birth certificate reads, "Immanuelis Cvi Mandel" (Emanuel Zvi in Hebrew). He was soon called Imi, a diminutive of Immanuelis that stuck with him until he arrived in America in March 1949. Imi remained an only child. This was not unusual for that period. During the time of the burgeoning unrest in Europe, many families chose not to bring children into the word. After World War II began, Lajos was often separated from Ella for long periods. Manny said, "I think they made a conscious decision not to have any more kids."

There were some complications with Lajos' papers which up to that time had disallowed him from working in Hungary. Nevertheless, in spring, 1936, he received notification that his case in Budapest was now in good order; he would be allowed to work there. Lajos later remarked: "So, I made plans to move to Budapest. Based on subsequent events, world war, the Holocaust, I should have taken the position in London. I should have gone to London. Why didn't I ?"

Lajos always let it be known that Budapest was his fervent desire. Having received a telephone call offering him a position

Imi, two years old, and maternal aunt, Magda.

in Budapest, the finest position any cantor could aspire to, he and Ella made plans to leave Riga. They both spoke Hungarian.

Imi, when he began to talk, would also speak Hungarian. Throughout the years, he would continue to converse in Hungarian with his mother. However, his father and he always spoke in the "language of the land."

In July of 1936, as the new *fokantor* at the Rumbach Temple, Lajos left for Budapest, where he immediately started to rehearse for the High Holy Days. He also had to consult extensively with the Choir Director, Dr. Revesz, about the selection of music.

Six weeks later, Ella's brother, Sanyi Klein, and her brother-in-law, Sanyi Hajdu, helped her pack and move so she could join her husband in Budapest. Imi was three months old.

At the time there were nearly two hundred thousand Jews in Budapest; they comprised fifteen to twenty percent of the population. The Mandels found accommodations in the older part of the new city of Pest—busier and more populous than Buda—within a mostly Jewish area, moving to a five story high-rise apartment at #13 Wessclenyi, two blocks from the Rumbach Synagogue, and five or six blocks from the Danube River. Lajos had rejected moving into a cheaper and smaller apartment next to the synagogue.

There were six to eight apartments per floor, three to four on each side of the elevator shaft. Each level of the apartment building had a balcony from which one reached their front double doors. On one of the doors, Lajos eventually posted a small sign: "Mandel, Chief Cantor." Inside, all of the ceilings were high, probably ten to twelve feet; the floors were of exposed wood, many covered with oriental rugs; the walls were overlaid with wallpaper, and many oil paintings.

Off of the foyer was a large wardrobe closet that would eventually hold Lajos's forty suits. He had so many suits because he needed different materials based on the season—spring, summer,

Imi with his parents, Ella and Lajos, Budapest, 1940.

fall, winter—and in between seasons. Besides, Lajos liked nice clothes. Manny always remembers his father as "a dapper man."

French doors led to the dining room, though the family ate there only on special occasions when Ella would use her hand-painted Rosenthal china. In addition to the table, the room also included a grand piano. The family had most of their meals in a day room. Off of a corridor there was a bathroom, which only contained a water closet, a toilet. Another bathroom had a tub, a shower, and a sink, but no toilet. There was a cooking kitchen with no seating, and a maid's room. A *uri szoba*, (gentlemen's room) sufficed as Lajos's study. The master bedroom contained twin beds and an additional bed. Manny said, "When my father's mother, Rosa, came to be with us, she would sleep in my bedroom, and I would sleep in the room with my mother and father."

The school Imi subsequently attended was at #44 Wesselenyi, just about four blocks from home. Within blocks of where they lived, there was a market, two synagogues, the banks of the Danube and a skating area. Lajos had no car, but then, very few people in Budapest owned a car. Travel was primarily by trolley, cab, bus, underground public transport or by horse-drawn carriage. Manny recalls that just before she died in Israel, Aunt Magda said, "One of the two things I regret not having done was to have gotten a driver's license."

According to need, there were synagogues in every district in Budapest. There were two *forebbes* (chief rabbis), and four *fokantors* (chief cantors), serving both major synagogues in Budapest. The two main places of worship are both in downtown Pest, are two blocks from each other, in the VII District—the Tabakh Temple on *Dohany Utca* (street) and the Rumbach Temple on *Rumbach Utca*. The Tabakh Temple, the largest synagogue in Europe, in many ways resembles a church basilica. It is situated on a corner and has two balconies with the *bimah* (raised platform) at one end. It holds three to five thousand people; its architecture is a traditional, Byzantine-Moorish style, with gilded onion-domed towers, brickwork of yellow, red and blue, and a large adjacent courtyard.

Situated in the middle of the block, the Rumbach Temple is

Lajos, Novi Sad 1932.

also Moorish in design. It is a semi-circular edifice with two towers that resemble minarets. One source says that "it was built, not as an exact replica of, but as homage to the octagonal, Dome of the Rock in Jerusalem." Constructed with eight sides, it is balconied, domed, inimically patterned and painted in Moorish style. There was a *bimah* in middle where the the Torah was the middle of the main sanctuary though there was another *bimah* closer to the arc.

Not nearly as imposing as the Tabak, the Rumbach is on a very narrow street. For crowd control police were brought in whenever services were held.

The Rumbach Temple was able to seat thirty-two hundred. Other than the seating capacity, there was, in Lajos's eyes, a major difference. The Tabak Temple had an organ, a long nave and pulpit, an eastern flavored interior and a mixed choir, while the Rumbach Temple had no organ. But it did have a forty voice male/child choir. As was the case in most of the synagogues in Budapest, the members of the Rumbach and the Tabak Synagogues were part of the Neolog community. Keeping the Jewish festivals, they attempted to fit in with the traditions of their fellow Hungarians.

Lajos, Budapest 1936.

The Neologs evolved as followers of the Mitnagdim whose leader, the *Vilna Gaon* (Sage of Vilna) emphasized, above all, intellectual Judaism. As was the case in most European synagogues of that time, there was no mixed seating and the congregation members were observant. When asked if he followed all 613 laws of the Torah, Lajos said, "I am observant, but not crazy." A portion of the community was orthodox. It included a Hasidic segment (A movement of popular mysticism founded in eastern Europe in the eighteenth century). Its founder was the *Ba'al Shem Tov* (Master of the Good Name).

The Jewish community ran its own hospitals, schools, and had its private cemetery.

All rabbis, cantors, doctors in the Jewish Hospital and other community employees negotiated with the Central Jewish Council. Taxes were collected by the government. Lajos was given a twenty-year contract, which would allow him to retire in his early fifties. Unfortunately, he would serve in that position for only ten years.

Lajos and Imi, Budapest 1941.

One of the reasons why he hadn't selected the Tabak Synagogue was because his mother would have objected to the organ. Even though the Rumbach Temple was Lajos's home synagogue, he often davened at the Tabak Synagogue. At age thirty-two, he was one of two *fokantors* at the synagogue; a man named Bornstein was the other cantor.

Traditionally, during the High Holidays, rabbis and cantors wear white. Lajos went all out; to some, he had a flair for the dramatic. Though, upon introspection, "He truly felt he was the voice of the congregation, the Jewish people carrying their voices to God." On Yom Kippur and Rosh Hashanah when he started singing the *Hineni* prayer ("the cantor's prayer"), dressed all in white (white jacket, white pants, white shoes and socks), he entered from the back of the synagogue and appeared quite impressive.

> *Here I am, utterly bereft, shuddering and afraid, in fear of the*
> *One who sits in judgement of the prayers of Israel.*
> *I have come to stand before You and plead on behalf of Your people,*
> *Israel, who have sent me, as unfit and unworthy as I am.*

Manny often speaks of his preferred celebration during his eight years spent living in Pest: "My favorite holiday was Simkhat Torah (the festival that comes at the end of Sukkot, and celebrates the completion of the annual cycle of Torah reading) because I got candy, but not because my cheek was pinched.

"I recall a Catholic family that lived in our building, also on the fifth floor. They had two girls—Baba and Katica. I vaguely remember playing with them. They had no concern about the yellow star. However, my uncle Dezso was my favorite; I adored him."

Imi spent his free time tinkering on the family piano—eventually he started taking piano lessons. Just prior to his fifth birthday, Manny was accepted at the Liszt Institute; Manny claims this was because he was left handed and could have a strong bass.

He learned to ice skate; the rink was only five blocks away from their apartment. "One weekday, my father took me skating. The congregation members, like most Hungarian Jews, were under the influence of Teutonic (German) traditions. One member complained: 'It isn't appropriate for the fokantor to take his son out.' Forabi Fisher took exception to this: 'Get off his back! If I was his age and I had a son, I would do the same thing.'"

Imi also learned to ride a bike, practice fencing, swim, frequently at a magnificent public swimming pool and, on occasion, in the dark waters of the Danube. Of course he learned to read and write, but now insists he has terrible handwriting. "I write with my right hand and throw with my left."

The family kept a kosher home, and on occasion, dined out at a kosher restaurant. Manny remembers "Weiss Kosher Restaurant, which was right across the street from our apartment. Dining out was not a regular activity in those days."

"When I was six, I turned over a chair in our dining room and gashed my groin. The pediatrician said, 'One centimeter more and you would have injured your reproduction system.'"

Manny also remembers his first opera: "Goldmark Hall, down the street from our apartment. It was Verdi's, *The Masked Ball*. I recall the King of Stockholm getting killed on the stage. This upset me very much, that is, until the actor took a bow at the end

left: Imi, cousin Judit (perished in Auschwitz), cousin Bata; Novisad
right: first day of school, Budapest 1943.

of the opera. My mother and father once took me to the Hungarian State Opera House. I remember the program was in two or three parts—the tragic one-act Italian opera, *Cavalleria Rusticana*, by Pietro Mascagni." Also on the program was Ravel's *Bolero* and a Hungarian folk opera.

"Many times I went to the old time, permanent circus and the zoo, famous for its art nouveau architecture. I was fascinated with the movies; when my Aunt Magda came to Budapest, she would take me to the movie theater.

"I did not attend Cheder. My school was, so to speak, a secular, Jewish school. My father often watched me on my way there and sometimes he even followed me when I walked to school. My world was the neighborhood; home, school, synagogue, the park, and the Danube.

"Father gave me my religious education; I never went to Hebrew school; he allowed me to live a secular life. We never really argued, though once we disagreed over the pronunciation of Levine. Then there was the time in our apartment when I was being very obnoxious; he spanked me on my behind. And another time he slapped my face; I've forgotten why.

"My mother and father once took me on a vacation to Balaton Lake, a freshwater lake in the Transdanubian region of Hungary. It's the largest lake in Central Europe. The day was overcast. Dad was reassured everything would be alright. It wasn't. A storm came up. It was treacherous, but we survived, ending up with my father dragging the boat to shore. "

In 1937, in both Hungary and Austria, anti-Semitic associations demanded the introduction of racist laws. Throughout Europe, many Jews began to live in a state of constant terror, though there was a sort of shrug-of-the-shoulder attitude in Hungary with many thinking "So what else is new?" One law instituted in Hungary, provided for "The More Efficient Protection of the Social and Economic Balance." The requirements embedded in this rather long-winded title limited Jewish participation in financial and productive employment. It also restricted Jews in the various professions.

In March of 1938, the Hungarian government commenced enforcing a succession of extremely harsh and discriminating "Jewish Laws." Jews were not allowed to hold positions in any government agency. They were no longer allowed to serve as physicians in hospitals. Those Jews who were not citizens of Hungary were either arrested or escorted to the borders. Fortunately, Lajos was given employment papers that allowed him to work as a non-Hungarian.

The government even got into the meat-making business. They decreed that all cattle were to be stunned before slaughter. This, of course, was directed against the Jewish community. *Shehitah* ritual, kosher slaughtering was prevented.

A law was enacted to reduce the number of Jews in the Hungarian business community to twenty percent over the next five years.

It was during this time, July 1938, that the unsuccessful Evian Conference on refugees took place, which aptly demonstrated what little chance there was for finding refuge for Jews in other countries. Earl Winterton, a representative of the British government, chaired the conference, which took place at the French resort town of Evian on the shores of Lake Geneva. He was not at all empathetic toward the Jews, and held a pro-Arab stance on Palestine. Another delegate, T.W. White, of Austria, chanced to remark: "It will no doubt be appreciated that as we have no racial problems we are not desirous of importing one." Several countries sealed off their borders; Britain, Palestine and the United States tightened their rules of admission. Argentina, Chile, Uruguay and Mexico adopted strict laws restricting the number of Jews who could enter their borders.

Two months later, Neville Chamberlain made an announcement while holding a worthless document signed by himself, Edouard Daladier, the Prime Minister of France, and Adolf Hitler at Munich declaring, "There will be peace in our time!"

There would be no peace; and Chamberlain's time was limited. This futile gesture allowed Hungary to violate their neighbors' frontiers, and gobble up territory it had lost in 1919 after the previous war. This included the Slovakian territories, home to 87,000 Jews.

On November 12, 1938, in Germany, Richard Heydrich demanded that Jews wear a badge for identification purposes. The following month, Dr. Hjalmar Schacht, the president of the Reichbank, proposed a package deal for the "liberation" of the Jews. He suggested a payment of three million marks ($1,200,000.00) tied together with a multifaceted scheme that would force the future émigrés to strengthen German exports, while they "reconstructed" their lives in other countries. The quid pro quo: fifty thousand Jewish workers would leave every year over a three-year period. Led by Assistant Secretary of State Sumner Wells, Jewish organizations in America condemned the Nazi offer. Wells said, "The plan is generally considered as asking the world to pay a ransom for the release of hostages in Germany and to barter human misery for increased exports."

Prime Minister Bela Imredy of Hungary asserted, "one drop of Jewish blood is sufficient to call into question an individual's character and patriotism!"

Because Hungary was now an ally of Germany, Jews were not allowed to serve in the army, and professionals couldn't practice their professions.

In 1942, the younger Jews, including Lajos, were organized into various slave labor battalions where they worked in factories, built roads and airports, worked on railroads, and did some coal and salt mining. Lajos was sent to various *munka tabors* (labor camps) for two weeks, sometimes three, sometimes a month, and occasionally three months. Lajos reported, "I was at home for four weeks, and sometimes away for two or more months. The winter months were easier; I could go home."

Rabbi Hevesi, chief rabbi of the Dohany Utca Synagogue suggested that Lajos become a chaplain in the labor forces. "That way, you won't be under the whip and will be entitled to certain privileges." It never happened.

One member of the Jewish community had a factory that made tin cans. Cooked food could be sent to the laborers in resealed cans. Ella often prepared tins of food, vacuum sealed, for Lajos in order to prevent botulism. Much of the Jewish leadership was at these labor camps. "Life, day to day, was acceptable. Life was as good as it can be, though the rules began to pinch," Lajos once commented.

Understatement was obviously one of Lajos's more apparent characteristics. Wearing civilian clothes with yellow arm bands, he and his fellow forced laborers often carried out dangerous assignments under filthy and exhausting circumstances. Sadistic guards, guns at the ready, oversaw their toil.

At first they served near their hometowns, but as the war progressed, by mid-1944, Lajos's labor battalion was relocated to the Ukraine. Home visits ceased.

Invariably undernourished and overworked, they sweated out the summer and froze during the winter. Sanitary conditions were nonexistent; medical care sparse. Later accounts reveal that of the hundred thousand forced laborers, sixty thousand survived.

Four

To Cantor Mandel, the glass was half full: "It was a terrible time, and worse, but [fortunately] I was still employed by the congregation." The Russians were now bombing Budapest forcing everyone to rush to the bomb shelters. Lajos helped repair the bomb damage in Budapest and the outskirts.

During Lajos's irregular pilgrimages to his labor battalion (1942-1944), he brought his mother, Rosa, to live with them; she had been a widow for over twelve years. Suffering from foot trouble, she first lived in her own apartment and soon after with them until early 1944. The five story apartment building was elevator equipped but it, like the building, was fifty years old.

When the elevator became inoperative, the repair parts needed were unavailable or had to be manufactured. The factories had been converted to the production of wartime materiel and elevator parts were low on the priority list. It was obvious that Mama, as she was called by the family, found it extremely difficult and eventually impossible to descend to the bomb shelter and then climb back up the stairs. Manny recalls that the privilege to call his grandmother "Mama" originated about that time when he was almost seven; it was a sign of his youthful maturity.

Lajos and Dezso thought it prudent to return Mama to their birth village, Csepe. While conditions there were primitive, it was free from air raids. However, as the Nazis occupied Hungary that spring and deportations started, Mama, with many others, was transported to Auschwitz where she was murdered. The actual date remains a mystery.

While a student at the University of Budapest, Dezso also lived with Lajos and Ella in their vintage early 1900s-era apartment. In 1944, wearing both tails and his yellow star, Dezso received his Doctor of Philosophy degree. Imi attended the graduation ceremony where he too wore a yellow star. Dezso had been a student at the University and at a Seminary in a combined program. Extremely knowledgeable in Hebrew grammar, which was the subject of his dissertation, he also taught Hebrew as part of a preparatory program for those making aliyah.

One of his students was Hannah Szenes (Senesh), one of Israel's national heroines, best remembered for her courage during the Holocaust and as a poet and martyr. In Randolph Braham's book, *The Tragedy of Hungarian Jewry: Essays, Documents, Depositions* (East European Monographs), Braham reproduces documents where Hannah refers to Dezso. Her mother remained in Hungary. In one of her letters home, Hannah asks that if her mother has contact with Dezso Mandel she should compliment him on his teaching because her language skills had become excellent.

Manny was told that Hannah would come to their apartment for her lesson, "say hello nice little boy, and pat him on the head." Of course, he does not remember. "She knew me. I did not know her," he explains, "because I was really a little boy."

Though safe in a Palestinian kibbutz during the war, Hannah

volunteered for a mission to rescue Jews in her native Hungary. After being parachuted into neighboring Yugoslavia on March 13, 1944, she and Yoel Palgi, a fellow Eretz Yisrael resident, separated so as to open up different routes of escape and rescue. Shortly after they had infiltrated their native land, Hannah and Palgi were both captured by the Nazis. She was imprisoned, tortured, and eventually executed. She was only twenty-three years old..

Step by duplicitous step, Hitler had called Britain and France's bluff. In 1935, breaking the Locarno Treaty, his armed forces had reoccupied the Rhineland. In 1937 the *Anschluss* (annexation) was underway, ending in the the bloodless takeover of Austria. The following year was the "road to Munich," an attempt at a peace treaty, but which culminated in the cutting up of Czechoslovakia by, not only Germany, but also Poland and Hungary (grabbing Ruthenia and Transylvania with its 72,000 Jews). What happened in 1939 was as foreseeable as it was inevitable. This would become a tragic denouement for the Jews.

The German Foreign Office, under the name "Schaumburg," issued a directive: "It is even today an important duty of German policy to control and when possible direct the flow of Jewish emigration to be sure there is no incentive to cooperate with other countries such as Poland, Hungary, and Rumania, who themselves are striving for the emigration of the Jewish sections of their population in an attempt to solve this problem."

Herman Goering delegated Helmuth Wohlthat, one of his advisors in the Ministry for Economic Affairs, to further pursue negotiations for Jewish emigration, knowing full well that there was no nation on earth willing to admit Jews in significant numbers. The lone Jewish newspaper still operating in Germany printed: "The United States, which initiated the Evian Conference, should be reminded of its moral duty to set other immigration countries a good example with a generous gesture. If the United States could decide to accept 100,000 Jews from Germany conditionally, they could remain in the thinly settled regions in the west of that country and would make a very valuable contribution to the solution of the emigration problem." The editors even mentioned the sparsely populated tundra of Alaska as a possible haven—a notion that was picked up by Michael Chabon in his novel, *The Yiddish Policeman's Union*.

Wohlthat let it be known to America's State Department that Germany was prepared to authorize an orderly emigration of its Jews. Representatives of German Jews were even allowed to go to London where they pled their case before the Intergovernmental Committee for immediate action, *vis-a-vis*, Jewish resettlement. America's State Department put a damper on the British proposal—the prospect of raising a hundred million dollars for refugee settlement over a five-year period—together, both governments would match the amounts raised by private subscription.

As Wohlthat laid out the specifics of the proposal, the exodus would commence with 150,000 wage earners from ages fifteen to forty-five, being permitted to emigrate during the next three to five years. During that transition, he reassured the world that there would be no new pressures or penalties against the remaining Jews. And in a gesture of further goodwill, he cynically announced that the wives, children and other dependants of the 150,000, would be allowed to join them. "The Third Reich will even retain emigrants for work in their new homes...Those Jews currently in concentration camps will be released once the program gets underway." As a final demonstration of Deutschland's benevolence, he added: "Germany will even rescind its twenty-five percent 'flight tax,'" This was a levy imposed on the Jews as they fled the Third Reich.

Acting as if the agreement suggested by Wohlthat had never been expressed, Goering announced a new diktat: All German or stateless Jews would surrender within two weeks, all jewelry and objects of gold, silver and platinum, including silver knives, forks and spoons.

By the end of February, the Jewish community was ordered by the police to provide the names of one hundred persons each day; those individuals would be required to leave Germany within two weeks! But where would they go? If they chose to remain in Germany they would be severely punished. There was, however, another caveat: These departing Jews would be forced to pay an amount equal to the value of any goods they wished to take with them.

On September 1, 1939, feigning provocation on the part of the Poles, Hitler invaded Poland from the air, land and sea (Westerplatte on the outskirts of Danzig), the first instance of what became known as *blitzkrieg* or "lightening war." Neville Chamberlain announced that Britain was now at war with Germany. The French waited a little longer, but soon joined the fray. The Russians invaded Poland from the East, occupying their pre-arranged share of the pie. World War II had begun.

In June of 1940, The United States Congress passed the Alien Registration Act, which effectively closed off all further immigration from Europe.

It didn't take long for Hans Frank, the chief of the Office of the Government General to announce that all Jews above the age of ten would henceforth wear a white armband with the Star of David on their right arm.

A year to the day after Germany had invaded Poland, by decree, badges were issued to the Jews within Germany as well as those Jews in occupied Poland. The badge was the yellow Star of David, with the word, "Jude" ("Jew") printed on it; it was to be worn at all times on the left side of one's chest. In April of 1942, Jews were ordered to paint the Star of David on their houses. The

Dezso Mandel, Imi's uncle, in
the Czech Army..

Yellow Star Decree was not published in Hungary until March,
1944.

Within months of the beginning of the war, Bergen-Belsen,
a prisoner of war camp, was established. The camp, which was
to play such a large part in Ella's, Imi's and Dezso's lives, is situated eleven miles south of the small towns of Bergen and Belsen,
approximately eleven miles north of Celle in Germany. Originally a POW camp, it was later added to the concentration camp
system and in addition to the POWs there was a *Aufenthaltslager,*
"residence camp," and a *Häftlingslager,* "prisoner's camp."

After he finished school, Dezso had no desire to join a religious movement. He wanted to become active in *Hashomer Hatzier,*
the Zionist youth movement, a left-wing group. In 1932, Dezso
had attended the Zionist Conference in Basel, Switzerland. In the
mid-1930s, Dezso spent considerable time in *hachshara* (training),
mostly in Munkach, then Hungary, now the Ukraine. This was
agricultural training for urban people who desired to form *aliyah*
groups in preparation to move to Palestine and establish *kibbutzim* on land acquired by the Jewish National Fund. Such groups
became the grounding for the future State of Israel. Most of Dezso's friends had made it to Palestine before the war.

In 1944, for the first time, he was called into a labor battalion, where, as it turned out, all of his service would be in territorial Hungary. Imi threw a tantrum, and Mama fainted. As Manny later described it: "Something was being excised from the family constellation." Dezso was to be married but his fiancée was later deported to Auschwitz; she did survive the war.

During the early days of the war (1940-1941), the Hungarian government shut down all Jewish newspapers, including *Uj Kelet* (The New East). During the day, Jews were not allowed to shop in stores; there was a specific time when they were allowed to shop but by then, the shelves were usually depleted. Ella's parents, who still lived in Novi Sad, sent whatever was needed to supplement provisions. Yehudah (Lajos) added: "They sent many things. Travelers from Novi Sad were assigned the task of making the deliveries."

Yehudah recalled some of his experiences: "We had the benefit of a big congregation, but the Arrow Cross came and functioned as though the 'laws' covered everything that could destroy Jewish life."

Manny commented on his own perspective as a child: "I didn't know what was happening to the Jews. However my father and mother weren't pleased with the soldiers and police. Contrary to my notion of how things were supposed to be, we were not rooting for the home team."

Manny had the impression that his parents had agreed not to bring another child into the chaotic world. Apparently other family members came to a similar conclusion. Ella was one of six children. Five (including Ella) were married. Between them they bore five children. One of Manny's four cousins perished in Auschwitz. Another three survived in Yugoslavia. Two of them still live in Belgrade. Manny never knew the one who had died. Ella's other sibling, a brother, married after the war and remained childless.

Between 184,000 and 246,000 Jews lived in Budapest at the start of 1941. In late summer, the Hungarian army expelled no less than twenty thousand Jews from conquered Ruthenia into the Ukraine, Soviet territory, which was, at the time, occupied by the Germans. All twenty thousand (another report says eleven thousand) were gunned down by SS troops; they were murdered in Carpathian Russia as German tanks pressed forward on the Ukrainian Plains.

In 1942, the Holocaust was now in full force. At Auschwitz, children up to twelve or fourteen, and older people (above fifty), as well as those who were sick, and people with criminal records, were, upon their arrival, taken immediately to the showers, which turned out to be gas chambers. All European Jews, save those in countries such as Hungary, which had allied itself to Germany, were included in the mass killing program. Chief responsibility for carrying out this draconian order was SS *Obersturmbannfuher* Adolf Eichmann, who headed up Gestapo Desk IV B4.

Prominent American Jewish leader, Rabbi Stephen Wise was told of Nazi plans to eliminate the Jews of Europe and passed this along to U.S. Undersecretary of State Sumner Wells, who in turn, asked for a detailed report of the situation. It documented that the liquidation of the Jews had already begun.

In December 1942, the SS, and its willing accomplices, had already executed over 1,450,000 Jews; approximately 600,000 of them were from occupied territories, and 800,000 were from the "integral" Soviet Union. Roosevelt and Churchill issued a joint public statement, revealing the dismal facts about the ongoing Nazi extermination program. They gave fair warning that all individuals engaged in such shocking activities would, at war's end, be tried as war criminals. However, at that time nothing else was done.

The *Va'adat Ha-Ezrah ve-ha-Hatzalah* (The Council for Assistance and Rescue) was organized and made up of Jews of varying political philosophies—Dr. Rudolf Rezso Israel Kasztner, a lawyer, headed up the group. Other leading principles were Joel and Hansi Brand, Otto Komoly, Moshe Krausz, and Eugen Frankel. Also in this eminent group was Ernest Szilagyi from *Hashomer Hatzair*. Functioning outside of formal Jewish institutions, the ad hoc committee personified a "daring and activist ethos," which the official Jewish Council lacked. That council had been set up under the aegis of the *Nyilas*. Very much cognizant of both work and deportation camps, the *Va'ada* was determined to aid their *landslaute* (fellow people), to save as many Hungarian Jews as possible, even though many still believed what had transpired in other European nations could never happen in a civilized country such as Hungary.

All of Europe was an inferno; its Jewish inhabitants were being laid waste. The *Va'ada* members realized that as long as there were 800,000 Jews alive in Hungary (Hungary's prewar population had nearly doubled because of the refugees fleeing the Nazis), Hitler and his henchman, Adolf Eichmann, would never be able to call Europe, *Judenrein* (free of Jews).

Kasztner devised a scheme. He and his group reached the ears of Adolf Eichmann who, at first, said he wanted "none of your little deals." But then, he suggested if *Va'ada* really wanted to cut a deal, he, Eichmann, would turn over to the committee one million Jews in exchange for ten thousand fully equipped winterized trucks with trailers that the Wehrmacht desperately needed.

Eichmann asked Brand, considered to be brave, intelligent and a bit of a swashbuckler, to broker a deal between the SS, the United States, and Britain. He repeated: "I'm prepared to release up to a million Jews who are otherwise destined for Auschwitz." He would do this if the Western allies would supply Germany with the ten thousand trucks, plus two million cakes of soap, two hundred tons of tea, two hundred tons of coffee, and an unspecified amount of tungsten and other war materials. This became known as the "blood for goods" (or merchandise) proposal. Kasztner, who felt he had negotiated entirely as an equal, said Eichmann guaranteed that the trucks for the Waffen-SS would only be used on the eastern front. Eichmann was posturing; his suggestion was farcical, especially his promise, on his word of honor, that the trucks would only be used to fight the Russians. Nonetheless, the parties were at least talking.

Years later, Kasztner, testifying in an Israeli court, said: "The Germans entered into discussion with leaders of the Jewish community for reasons of administrative efficiency. We conducted the discussion in hopes that we might be able to save some human lives. By holding the ax over our heads, they made us responsible for financial contributions and other exactions imposed on the Jewish community. Ultimately the leaders of the 'Jewish Council' and other intermediaries were also scheduled for extermination. The SS and the Gestapo were particularly intent on liquidating those who had direct knowledge of their operations.

"I escaped the fate of the other Jewish leaders because the complete liquidation of the Hungarian Jews was a failure and also because SS Standartenfuehrer Becher took me under his wings in order to establish an eventual alibi for him. He was anxious to demonstrate after the fall of 1944 that he [disapproved of] the deportations and exterminations and endeavored consistently to furnish me with evidence that he tried to save the Jews. SS Hauptsturmfuehrer Wisliceny repeatedly assured me that according to him Germany couldn't win the war. He believed that by keeping me alive and by making some concessions in the campaign against the Jews he might have a defense witness when he and his organization will have to account for their atrocities. Strangely, he came to Hungarian Jews with the letter of recommendation from leading Slovak Jews. The latter were not deported in 1942 and were saved until the end of 1944."

Kasztner contacted many wealthy Hungarian Jews. After reasoning and cajoling, he was able to raise the equivalent of a million dollars. The stage was set for the first part of a bargain:

"The original proposal was reduced, changed, adjusted many times. Nothing really moved; there were continual delays. At one point it was $1,000.00 up to $2,000.00 per head (some paid more, some less; it was not necessarily in currency, but could be in jewels or other precious items) to send them to a neutral port. This was for those in Hungary who held valid exit visas during the war. If they didn't have them, they could be printed. Everything had to be legal; anything that was stamped and in triplicate was okay by the Germans. It was not a noble process, but had to do with who could raise the money and had enough pull. Exodus was arranged, ransomed, or bought."

Kasztner agreed to explore the possibility of a deal with the Americans. For the initial contact, he selected Istanbul, Turkey, the eye of the needle for spying. Kasztner sent Brand, who was accompanied by a Nazi agent, acting as Eichmann's eyes.

Of all the *Va'ada* chieftains Kasztner remains an enigma to this day. Some say he wanted "greater glory." Others praise him, and still others damn his questionable practices. One would later vilify him in the press, and a court ruled against him. Finally a group took matters into its own hands and assassinated him. To this day there are those who say the *Va'ada*, actually Kasztner, failed to warn the Jewish community of the ongoing Holocaust, the true nature of Auschwitz and other concentration camps. They were fearful that passing on this knowledge would compromise and end their negotiations with Eichmann. In truth, this information was available to many. By the spring of 1944, the death camps were common knowledge throughout most of Hungary. Many simply didn't want to acknowledge the evidence. After all, what kind of individuals would do such a thing to other human beings? For what? Being a Jew?

In what seems like a "march of idiocy," events were happening at a furious pace: On March 18, 1944, Regent Admiral Miklos

Horthy and his staff were summoned to Germany; a stormy meeting with Hitler ensued. The next day, Sunday, March 19th, German troops began to occupy Hungary. Splitting hairs, they never physically "invaded" Hungary; the Arrow Cross were capable of doing their own dirty work. Heretofore, since Hungary was allied with the Germans, there were few Germans in Hungary.

Within three weeks, approximately six thousand individuals, mostly Jews, were removed from Hungary. On the 19th, Eichmann arrived in Budapest with the troops, and established his headquarters in the Majestic Hotel. A Fascist government was set up; members of the organization known as "Spearhead," were immediately appointed directors of the section dealing with the Jews in the Ministry of the Interior. Thus far, Hungary was not ghettoized; internal traffic was not completely restricted, and it was mostly on foot.

Soon SS Hauptsturmfuehrer Dieter Wisliceny arrived in Budapest to facilitate the Jewish deportation.

After the German army occupied Hungary, Miklos Horthy chose Dome Sztojay as the new prime minister and removed Prime Minister Miklos Kallay from office. Under his control, a cabinet of Quislings—traitors who serve as puppets of the enemy occupiers of his country—was formed; its prime purpose was the solution of the Jewish problem. One anti-Jewish decree followed another.

As prime minister, Sztojay was essentially a marionette of The Third Reich. He filled his cabinet with fascists such as Bela Imredy, legalized Ferenc Szalasi's fascist Arrow Cross Party, increased the Hungarian military on the Eastern Front, gave notice to the nation's labor unions, imprisoned political opponents, cracked down on left wing politicians and activists. Sztojay refused to kowtow to Horthy's authority. He then carried out substantial persecutions of Jews, which, within two months, was to spiral into deportations to concentration camps.

President Roosevelt issued a statement condemning the Nazis for their crimes: "As a result of the events of the last few days, hundreds of thousands of Jews who, while living under persecution, have at least found a haven from death in Hungary, and the Balkans, are now threatened with annihilation as Hitler's forces descend more heavily upon these lands."

At the request of the German General Staff, the whole of Ruthenia, Upper Hungary and Northern Transylvania were declared "operational territory," which was another way of saying Germany would now be fighting on their ally's turf.

It took little time from Eichmann's arrival in Budapest before the yellow star, ghettoization laws, and deportation were fully enacted.

"From our home's window," said Manny, "you could see the Jewish elementary school where I received my education. It was a modern school in a big city. I remember air raid drills, and singing songs.

"The concentric circles grew tighter and tighter but attempts at resistance increased. When it was Dezso's turn to set up the illegal printing press for reproducing documents; it was moved around.When it was at our apartment, it was hidden in the music room, which also served as my bedroom. Sometimes I was evicted from my bedroom. I slept on a couch in my parents' bedroom."

On April 5, a German regulation was put in place, compelling every Jew to wear a yellow Star of David on his or her coat.

When the Yellow Star Decree was published, Imi Mandel also had to wear one.

"I considered it as a badge of honor and courage —a mark of distinction," he recalls. "To me that was terrific. Here I am, just like all the adults. They had yellow stars, and I have a yellow star. I lost it after the war during one of our moves.

"In an ongoing progressive dwindling of rights, a man came

to the house and said, 'I must take your telephone.' It was tak-
en away. We had to tell our maid, Margit, to go. She was an
eighteen-year-old farm girl of sturdy peasant stock. She was my
friend and she wanted to take me with her to her village to protect me from the Nazis and the unsavory, fascist-leaning Hungarians." Manny's mother would not agree to such a proposal.

Later, Yehudah recalled that "Jews were forbidden to visit
public places such as parks, restaurants and swimming pools.
Jews were not allowed to employ Christians, nor could they have
servants. We were not even allowed to use a public telephone.
Jews who broke the rules would be deported."

Clearly, the yellow star was an important symbol in Imi's
rudimentary recognition of the events of the day. Having
thought of the star as a mark of honor, he was rudely awakened
to its real meaning with an incident both he and his father remembered. Imi had approached his father with the request for
a new bicycle. He could not use a full size but there were bikes
appropriate for his size available to replace his tricycle. His father told him that there were two hindrances to the purchase;
economic reasons were not a concern. Living on the fifth floor
without a consistently working elevator, the bike would have to
be carried downstairs, taken to the park nearby, ridden and then
the process reversed. Imi, at the age of not yet eight, might have
problems accomplishing this but his father said that, while oner-
ous, this was a task he could perform.

However, the second reason was a deal-breaker. Since Imi
would have to ride the bike in the park and could be out of his
father's sight for a short time, someone could look at him wearing the yellow star and knock him off the bike. This would be an
act of hostility toward the star and Imi would be the target. Such
events happened and Imi would be placed in jeopardy. No bike!

Much later, in 1949, shortly after their arrival in New York,
the family went shopping. One of the first items purchased for

Manny was a brand new Schwinn, the standard, quality bicycle of the time.

The beginning realization of the meaning of the star and the events around Imi had made an impression. At a very young age, they were his first elements of understanding about world/ Jewish realities. He could not have understood all of the dangers present but was not totally immune from its effects. He said, "When I was seven and wearing my yellow star, some Gentile strangers 'brushed' past me. The yellow star was a target, but much less so in the 7th district. It was dicey, not pleasant."

On April 3, 1944, the Allies bombed the capital for the first time, the initial air raid hitting the southern part of Budapest. From then on, night and day, British and American planes bombarded the industrial areas. The Russian had been bombing for some time.

At Dr. Ernst Kaltenbrunner's (head of the RSHA—Reich Main Security Office), urging, Prime Minister Sztojay agreed that Hungary would place three hundred thousand Jewish workers at the disposal of the Reich; they were to be selected by a mixed Hungarian-German committee.

Higher SS and Police leader for Hungary, Otto Winkelmann, and Reich Ambassador, Edmund Veesenmayer were dispatched to visit various officials in the Hungarian Government, warning them not to interfere with the deportations that Eichmann was already planning. Veesenmayer was also working behind the scenes to remove Horthy from power, consolidating all power under the Arrow Cross, and ultimately the Nazis.

Eichmann met with Laszlo Endre, and Laszlo Baky, both from the Hungarian radical right and avid anti-Semites, at the Ministry of the Interior and planned the total deportation of all Jews. The rounding up of the Jews in the villages around the city began; they were to be forced into urban areas.

Fokantor Lajos Mandel was asked by Mr. Epler, the Secretary General of the Rumbach congregation if he could help him out in the 7th District.

"People had been thrown out of their homes, and thrown together willy-nilly: the old, the young, the kosher and non-kosher. There were some districts where Jews couldn't live at all. I organized the 7th District. I determined who was a Jew, and who was not a Jew [by that, he meant, who kept a kosher home, and who didn't]. We were allowed by the Germans and the Arrow Cross to do this for quite a while. It was preparatory for the ghettos," Yehudah recalled.

A meeting was arranged between Dr. Kasztner, Mr. Brand, another representative of the *Va'ada*, and Eichmann. It was held in Eichmann's office at the Majestic Hotel.

"You know who I am," said Eichmann to Joel Brand. "I am the man who liquidated the Jews of Poland, Slovakia, and Austria, and now I have been appointed head of the liquidation commando in Hungary. I am willing to do business with you—human lives for merchandise. What do you want? Woman who can bear children? Men who can make them? Children? Whatever is left of your people's biological potential?"

The first deportation took place on April 23. Fifteen hundred men suitable as laborers were taken from the Kistarca Internment Camp to Auschwitz. The War Refugee Board sent a direct message to Pope Pius XII. The Board urged him to intervene personally and to threaten the Nazi partners-in-crime with excommunication. Come May, the pace picked up. Cossacks were in the Ukraine and in the foothills of the Carpathians. A secret decree was issued ordering the establishment of ghettos in different parts of Hungary.

Kasztner and many other Jewish leaders knew that Jews were being sent to their deaths, having received the Vrba-Wetzler report known as the "Auschwitz Protocol" from two Serbian Jews, Rudolf Vrba (originally Walter Rosenberg) and Alfred Wetzler. Both had escaped from Auschwitz on April 7, later hiding out in Slovakia. Their report was eventually reported in the Swiss press and printed by the War Refugee Board in America, but not until November of 1944.

Eichmann advised Brand that deportations to Auschwitz were about to begin at the rate of twelve thousand Jews a day but he assured him that they would not be exterminated while negotiations were ongoing. Eichmann summoned Brand and Kasztner for a talk. Krumi (Scherzer) Schreber, and Willi, all members of the Gestapo, took part in the discussion. Eichmann bragged that he had already executed three and a half million Jews. If the Jews so desired, he would now be willing to make a deal with them: goods instead of blood. Would they be willing to exchange Jews for German POWs? It was the first of three or four talks. They said they were willing to deliver the Jews to the border of Spain or Portugal. One of them blurted that they would also want a little money. "We will release one hundred Jews for each truck delivered to us."

Monsignor Angelo Roncalli (later Pope John XXIII) forwarded thousands of baptismal certificates to Papal Nuncio Angelo Rotta in Hungary. Finally, the Pope sent a personal plea to Admiral Horthy. However, 437,402 Jews had already been recorded as having been deported on one hundred twenty trains from Hungary to Auschwitz. There were forty-five cattle cars in each train; each car contained an average of 70 Jews; they shared one bucket of water. The exact numbering of each car was marked in chalk on the outside. In a typical day, 12,000 Jews were delivered to Auschwitz. Historians contend that one third of the murdered victims at Auschwitz were Hungarian.

On May 17, the SS drove Brand and Bandi Grosz (Andre

Antol Gyorgy) to Vienna where they stayed the night in a hotel
reserved for SS personnel. Arriving in Istanbul, they hoped to
meet Moshe Sharett (then Shertok) of the Jewish Agency but this
did not happen. The original destination was Cairo to discuss
trucks with the British. Brand was arrested by the British in Al-
lepo and soon held in Cairo where he met Lord Moyne, the British Deputy Resident Minister of State in the Middle East. Moyne
was quoted as saying, "What can I do with this million Jews?
Where can I put them?"

A backup for Brand was made available. Chiam Barlacz,
the Chief Delegate of the Jewish Agency (JOINT) in Turkey, sub-
stituted for him. Ambassador Lawrence Steinhardt, also a Jew,
met with Barlacz who passed on Eichmann's proposition. Enter FDR—the President sent Ira Hirschmann, Vice President of
Bloomingdale's Department Stores, to Istanbul to listen to the
story first-hand. The deal was stillborn. After locking up Brand,
the British let it be known, especially to Stalin, that they had refused even indirectly to deal with Eichmann.

At the same time, at a meeting of the Jewish Agency Executive in Jerusalem, they voted to send Shertok to Turkey. They also
determined that they should announce that the negotiations were
ongoing and they should see if they could turn the negotiations
into money, not goods. Their comrades in Istanbul were instruct-
ed to insist on an immediate halt to the deportations. The goal was
to buy time in order to rescue Jews from the inferno that Europe
had become.

Ambassador Steinhardt agreed to meet with Brand once he
arrived in Ankara. This was likely a foolish move because if the
Russians ever got wind of such a conversation, they were sure
to conclude that America was about to stab them in the back.
The Russians were masters of the art of the double cross, having
crawled into bed with Hitler before castrating Poland. To many,
a distrustful British government and the lethargy of the Jewish

Agency thwarted the "blood for goods" proposal. While this was going on, Hansi Brand (Joel's wife), still in Hungary, was arrested and beaten, a *de rigueur* activity in those chaotic days.

Early in the summer of 1944, Kasztner met with Eichmann in Budapest. A mini-version of the proposal was agreed upon for fifteen hundred (it ultimately became more) Jewish men, women, and children to be saved for a yet unspecified amount of money per Jewish person. Kasztner would have to raise a fortune to pass on to Eichmann. The chosen would board a "specially chartered train," no doubt consisting of box cars—passenger trains were constantly ferrying troops about—that would allow them to disembark at some, as yet undetermined safe haven. Despite innumerable glitches and complaints from both sides, the rescue plan proceeded.

In January of 1942, Eichmann had participated in the Wannsee conference convened by Reinhard Heydrich, where the "Final Solution" of eleven million Jews living in Europe and Russia was discussed, contrived and disseminated. Now, more than two years later, Eichmann, even though given specific guidelines by SS Chief Heinrich Himmler, was "sticking his neck out;" he would have a personal stake in the fate of this particular transit group.

Five

How does one select up to 1,685 Jews out of a nation of plus or minus 825,000 Jews—185,000 in Budapest alone? The method of selection mixed morality with ethics, affairs of state, with expediency, along with a measure of compassion. Kasztner first selected his wife and close relatives, many of whom were rich Hungarian Jews who were in turn able to subsidize some of their poorer brethren, others who could afford it, and then their wives and children. Who else would go, and how would they be selected?

At the same time these negotiations were transpiring, in June of 1944, Hungarian authorities ordered Budapest's Jews into over two thousand designated buildings scattered throughout the city. Each building was marked with a Star of David.

Concomitantly, approximately twenty five thousand Jews from the suburbs of Budapest were immediately rounded up, and transported directly to the Auschwitz-Birkenau extermination camp.

While the train negotiations were transpiring, Kasztner,

representing the *Va'ada* in the capacity of executive director, met with Eichmann and Dieter Wisliceny, Eichmann's representative in Hungary. On June 3rd, they tried to negotiate the release of another group, some six to eight hundred Jews from the provinces to the relative safety of Budapest. Kasztner said to Wisliceny: "The Rescue Committee is ready to deal 'in economic terms' with the Sonderkomando in order to 'mitigate the Jewish distress.'" As the result of the negotiations, an additional fifteen thousand Hungarian Jews were transferred to labor camps at Strasshof, near Vienna. At least for the time being, this saved them from Auschwitz.

Kasztner was fluent in five languages: Hungarian, Romanian, French, Latin, and German. Looking directly into Kasztner's shrewd eyes, Eichmann said in German: "Your nerves are too tense, Kasztner. I shall send you to Theresienstadt, or perhaps you prefer Auschwitz." He went on: "You must understand me. I have to clean up the provincial towns of their Jewish garbage. I must take this Jewish muck out of the provinces. I cannot play the role of the savior of the Jews."

Still, Kasztner, who had been a Zionist since he was fifteen, was able to strike another deal with the dangerous German; eighteen thousand Jews, mostly from Budapest were moved to a labor camp. Some fifteen thousand of them were still alive in 1945. Eichmann also agreed to transport a train full of Jews to Spain, as "a sign of good faith."

Kasztner had a reputation for being insensitive toward other people; he didn't care whether or not he alienated his friends. He was a political fixer, a wheeler-dealer, and had little patience for the niceties of behavior.

When a film, *Killing Kasztner*, produced by filmmaker Gaylen Ross, was premiered in New York City in 2010, Manny was invited to attend. He was interviewed by a *New York Times* reporter and asked about his reaction to Kasztner.

Manny made clear that, of course,as a child, he had no contact with the man, but his father knew him. Based on that and other reports, Manny felt that he would not have seen Kasztner as someone with whom he would have established a relationship. Kasztner was a *boulevardier* who frequented coffee houses and always wanted to live what today might be called a "jet-set" life. However, if not for this part of his personality, Kasztner could have never faced Eichmann, negotiated with him and saved more Jewish lives than any other Jewish person.

Kasztner knew who to bribe, who to pay off, how much to pay, and who to flatter; he could be charming if necessary.

Though he would remain behind in Hungary, he managed to survive the war and was eventually reunited with his wife. To those he had helped save, he was a hero. Others were not nearly as generous. Many people felt he had "sold his soul to the devil," and condemned him for leaving so many behind—although some did survive.

In retrospect, it was conjectured by some, including Malkiel Greenwald (Kasztner's future accuser in Israel), that the *Va'ada's* voluntary collaboration with the authorities, combined with the ignorance of the Jews themselves, facilitated and indeed enabled the deportation of several hundred thousand Jews from Hungary to Auschwitz in Poland. Why? It was argued that none of this could have happened without the voluntary collaboration on the part of people like Kasztner, and the Va'ada. Collaboration, an ugly word, has never been defined. Suffice it to say, negotiations can not take place in a vacuum. Contact between Kasztner and Eichmann *had* to take place in order to save Jews.

By the end of May 1944, 217,000 Hungarian Jews had been deported to Auschwitz. By June 3, another 253,389. On June 6, D-Day, when the allies invaded the Normandy beachheads, deportations to Auschwitz-Birkeneu were completed—some 437,000 (one source says 475,000) Hungarian Jews had been locked in enclosed railroad cars and sent to the death camp. Upon their arrival, the Nazis chose who would immediately be sent to be gassed in a huge underground chamber. Others were spared, at least temporarily, to work or serve other purposes.

It was also in early June that Hannah Szenes was hoping to secretly cross into her native Hungary.

Eichmann was still working on his "trucks for lives' deal," and pressuring Kasztner, saying: "If I do not receive a positive reply within three days, I shall operate the mill at Auschwitz."

By organizing this special rescue train for Kasztner and other Jews, including his relatives and friends, the Nazis were "generously" offering, for a handsome ransom, the "gift of life." The price finally arrived at was a thousand dollars (some accounts say two thousand dollars) per head. The group's leaders had in fact already given Eichmann and his gang a large part of the ransom, which had been paid by numerous individuals in currency (pengo and dollars), banknotes, jewels, platinum, gold cigarette boxes, gold coins, suitcases full of gold, diamonds and other valuables. Much of the money had been collected by selling seats to wealthy Jews. Kasztner auctioned off one hundred fifty seats to wealthy Jews to pay for the others, at between one to two thousand dollars per head. Some rich individuals contributed five-thousand dollars, others more, some less. Of course they—the financers—would also be on the train.

An envoy from Heinrich Himmler insisted that fifty seats be reserved for families of individuals who had personally paid him money for an assortment of special treatments; he wanted $25,000.00 per head. *Standartenfuehrer* Kurt Becher said to Kasztner: "There will be fifteen hundred Jews on board. I want fifty, well maybe one hundred seats. I will let you know." He later assured Kasztner: "Your train will be safe."

The total value of the ransom was estimated to be the equivalent of 8,600,000 Swiss francs, though Becher, a longstanding adversary of Eichmann, valued it at "only" 3,000,000 francs. After the war, Kasztner hoped that the ransom could be returned to some Jewish organization, and then perhaps distributed to the original contributors. However, the value remaining in the boxes was estimated at approximately $65,000.00, as opposed to a German (Becher and Schweiger) estimate of what they professed to have been (when it left their hands), two million dollars.

Years later, while on trial in Israel, after he had been captured by the Mossad, Eichmann said Kasztner "agreed to help keep the Jews from resisting deportation—and even keep order in the collection camps—if I could close my eyes and let a few hundred or a few thousand young Jews emigrate [sic] illegally to Palestine. It was a good bargain. For keeping order in the camps, the price...was not too high for me... We trusted each other perfectly.... Dr. Kasztner's main concern was to make it possible for a select group of Hungarian Jews to emigrate to Israel.... I believe that Kasztner would have sacrificed a thousand or a hundred thousand of his blood to achieve his political goal...'You can have the others,' he would say, 'but let me have this group here.' And because Kasztner rendered us a great service by helping keep the deportation camps peaceful, I would let his group escape."Eichmann spoke of Kasztner as "an ice-cold lawyer, and a fanatical Zionist.

"After all, I was not concerned with small groups of a thousand or so Jews... That was the 'gentleman's agreement' I had with Kasztner." In a revealing moment, Eichmann also said, "Dr. Kasztner had sacrificed his fellow Jews to my 'idea' [saving the best biological material, 'valuable Jewish blood'] and this was as it should be."

One wonders how much of this was fabricated or self-serving though it does have the flavor of truth. What is undeniable is that Eichmann and his staff had gone to great pains to make sure the Jews were not informed of the real destination of the trains.

By June 10, 1944, Kasztner had selected fifty-two immediate family members, including his mother and brother, 388 of his own extended family, as well as groups of family friends. The ruling Jewish party (made up of a community of Zionist leaders who had devoted their lives for the revival of Eretz Yisrael) made the decision as to who could go and who had the money to pay for their trip. Besides the people who paid the ransom out of their own resources, the assemblage included holders of immigration certificates who had been chosen on the recommendation of the Palestinian office; survivors from outlying cities; revisionists; refugees from Poland, Slovakia and Yugoslavia who had been selected by their representatives; liberal Jews selected by Samuel Stern, the head of the Jewish Council; widows; women whose husbands had been taken away to forced labor camps; children, especially orphans, forty of them; individuals who had served the Jewish community and were involved with Jewish social causes; forty rabbis and rich members of the Orthodox community chosen by Rabbi Freudiger. There were also several physicians, intellectuals, writers, journalists, farmers, landowners, former officers in the Hungarian army, ladies of leisure, scientists, two opera singers, and artists chosen by a committee chaired by Otto Komoly.

The Mandels were allotted four spots; if Lajos had been there, it would probably have been five. The four were eight-year-old Imi, his mother Ella, Imi's Uncle Dezso (then in his late twenties), and a first cousin, Dushko, the son of Lajos' younger brother, Bela (Vijoslav) Mandel, a cantor in Vukovar.

Younger than Imi, Dushko was not registered with the local police. It would have taken two months for him to get his certification; besides, he didn't speak Hungarian and this worried everyone. Dushko was sent back to Vukovar to wait. He was soon deported to Auschwitz with his mother, never to be seen again.

Days before departure, Magda Fleishmann came to the Mandel apartment and asked Imi's mother to take her son, Ivan, then four years old, instead of the deported Dushko. Magda's husband, Dr. Imre Fleishman, a veterinarian, was Dushko's mother's brother.

Ivan, eventually known as Yoash in Palestine, would become Manny's temporary brother . Yoash's parents survived the war and the family was reunited. Yoash, his wife and children currently live in Omer, Israel.

As an ardent Zionist, Dezso had many connections; he worked in the underground illegally, and had attended the Basel World Zionist Conference in 1932. He was affable, articulate and politically astute and was probably very much responsible for the Mandels being allotted four spots; at the time, his fiancé was living in Ungvar. Even though Lajos was away at the time, his position as *Fokantor* of the Rumbach synagogue was certainly a factor. Besides, the family was not poor. Lajos had a relatively high ministerial salary, and had also invested in Erno Krishaber's (Ilonas' husband) leather factory. Lajos also earned money from his concerts.

The Krishaber's factory became a family investment. It was located in Ruma, Yugoslavia near Novi Sad. As Eichmann subsequently cleared the area of Jews, Erno, Ilona and Yudit were given one day to leave. All investments were lost. Yehuda later mused, "The money would have bought me an orchard in Palestine — for my retirement."

Another youngster, about the same age as Imi, was Shaul Ladany. He recalls that his father was "a Zionist activist since his student years at the University of Karlsruhe in Germany, and also in Hungary during the war years, and as such he was selected to be included in the first transport of the Kasztner train."

Shaul's father's parents and sister were not included. They were selected for the second and third group that also assembled in the Columbus Street Camp in Budapest in in anticipation of more transports under the framework of "ten thousand trucks for one hundred thousand Jews." But Joel Brand's mission to Turkey and Palestine failed. After the German guards that protected the camp disappeared, the remaining groups were left to their own devices; they left the [Columbus Street] Camp and sought refuge at some other place.

Years later, Shaul and his mother went to visit in Hungary his paternal grandparents and cousins that had survived the war. The rest of his family were gassed in Auschwitz. Shaul and his mother were able to retrieve some of the furniture that her husband's parents had recovered.

Shaul is now a retired professor at Ben Gurion University in Israel. Manny remembers him well in Bergen-Belsen and later in the Heiden, Switzerland children's home.

Julie Spiegel Goldman said that her parents and maternal grandfather, Geza Boschan, owned and operated a large men's clothing store in Kolozsvar, Hungary. They were very active in the Jewish community and were members of the Jewish Council in Kolozsvar. The four members of the Spiegel family were selected and, no doubt, paid to be on the train. Prior to their departure, some non-Jewish Hungarians came to their home and demanded all of their possessions, money and valuables. Seven-year-old Julie went into her purse and handed them the few *pengos* she had.

Also in the Kasztner group was the *Satmar* Rebbe, Rabbi Yoel Teitelbaum. A brilliant scholar, he was an anti-Zionist, and vehemently opposed the creation of the State of Israel, insisting that it must wait for the coming of the Messiah. He wound up living in the Williamsburg section of Brooklyn, New York where he reestablished the *Satmar* Hasidic movement.

As a result of further negotiations, the *Sondergruppe* (special group) would be allowed to leave for a neutral port, claiming to be displaced persons during the war. Everyone claimed that they had papers to prove this fallacy. In reality, these were Jewish National Fund certificates.

Ella, like countless others, wondered whether or not she'd ever see her husband again. While, at a labor camp, Lajos was in a similar state: "I could not forget Ella and Imi and my brother, Dezso."

Ella had gotten Imi a pair of handcrafted ankle boots, which had wooden dowels on the bottom that attached the shoes together This was a typical manufacturing method in Europe. They were dressed in their traveling clothes, and brought along other necessities. They were allowed two changes of clothing, six sets of underwear, and enough food for a ten-day journey. In the beginning, based on the exit papers everyone held, Ella thought they might be headed to Spain, Turkey or even Germany for passage to Palestine.

Ella had packed a liter bottle of honey, a bottle filled with *schmaltz* (chicken fat), and a large slab of a bacon/ham-like smoked substance. Even though they kept a strictly kosher home, emergencies allowed certain "deviations." Ella knew that these items were nourishing, and didn't require refrigeration. These items were to last the length of their journey to any eventual destination.

There was a sense of "dulled excitement." One person had brought a sextant, another a compass, others carried a variety of valuables for trade; everyone carried with them some food. Imi brought along his two prize books, *Tamas Batya Kunyhoja* and *Robinson Crusoe Kalandjai.* Fortunately, while on the train, there would be no shortage of food. Ella had a diamond ring with her, which she hid in a bar of soap before they left. She knew it might become useful in a future barter.

The time for their departure finally arrived. To Imi it seemed like an exciting trip. "Mother told me we were being deported. I wasn't sure what that was, only that we were leaving. It sounded like an adventure, but Mother said it was serious."

To Ella, there was fear of the unknown and also of the known. At the time, Lajos was in Vac (Vacz), a town in Pest County, Hungary, twenty-two miles north of Budapest on the eastern bank of the Danube, in the foothills of the Carpathians. Up to that time all of the labor camps where Lajos had worked were in territorial Hungary.

On June 30, 1944, walking five rows abreast in a heavy rain, they were on there way to the *Rakorendezo* Railway Station. Ella said to Imi, "Wipe the smile off your face!" And when they got onto a horse drawn wagon, she said: "Don't look at this as a happy adventure!"

At the railway station, where uniformed guards looked on, they were crowded into a German freight train, not a passenger troop train, approximately eighty people to one of thirty-five boxcars. The first car was set aside for the "leaders" and their families; the second for those who were ill; the third for SS guards; and the fourth for supplies. The compartments of the "cattle cars" were reasonably clean with straw on the floor. The doors were shut after them, but not padlocked; when the train would stop, they would be allowed to get out for rest stops. Suitcases and food were packed into wagons attached to the end of the train. There were a few makeshift benches; most of the passengers either stood or settled on the floor of the train, surrounded by their bags. Each boxcar had a single bucket containing fifteen to twenty liters of water, and another bucket that served as a toilet. A major distraction was the crying of babies. Some men smoked and whiled away the time sitting on the window ledges, their legs dangling their feet over the outside of the compartment. Meat, tinned meat, cheese, jam and bread were handed out to the passengers. During the arduous trip, many people felt faint, became sick and vomited.

Ella soon discovered everybody in the group was not an honorable scout. One of the first things she did during their nine day journey on the train was to hide her soap. Shortly thereafter she realized the soap was stolen and, along with it, her diamond ring. Jews became thieves—it seemed like often those who were the wealthiest during normal times were the worst offenders.

The train didn't leave until after an air raid, at 11:00 PM. They circled the city for the entire first day and returned to where they had begun. What did that mean? Fear permeated the group. What they hadn't realized was that, during the night, the train had moved to the outskirts of the city, and stopped at a siding where it took on more coal.

By this time, the family had been reduced. Lajos's brothers, Jeno and Bela, Ella's brothers-in-law, Sanyi and Erno, as well as her parents, all from Yugoslavia, were murdered in Auschwitz or in forced labor camps.

Even though the train group was being deported "by choice," they were concerned whether or not they could trust their decision. A half hour after midnight, July 1, they started off again. This time, they were reassured when they were able to determine that they were headed north.

Because there were no real sanitary facilities on the train, they were forced to urinate in a corner of the car. At other times they relieved themselves in an observation structure atop the car that overlooked the countryside. Defecation was a real problem—people remembered the awful smell.

During the trip, there was a two day stop when the group left the train, gathered in a field and watched while British planes heavily bombed a nearby town. They were guarded by German soldiers but were able to dig a latrine far from the train and build a plank fence to conceal it. On the fourth day, their last in Hungary, as they moved into Austria, a woman gave birth to a baby in one of the boxcars.

They were informed that they would be able to take showers in Auspitz, a city that sounded too much like Auschwitz. Some aboard were not unfamiliar with the gas "showers" at the death camp in Poland. Panic set in. Julie Spiegel's father knew, but had kept the information from his wife. He and other individuals on the train bribed the conductor to stop the train due to some malfunction. They sent word back to Kasztner in Budapest. They received a reassuring response, and the journey continued without any showers in Auspitz.

The showers that awaited them in Linz were real enough, but hardly pleasant. Each individual was required to stand naked in front of a German doctor, disinfected and sprayed with disinfectant before being allowed to take his or her communal "hot" shower—forty to fifty men men and women together, overseen by guards. At first, thinking they might be gassed, there was much screaming.

At one point, the train stopped at the Vienna station, where, from the roof of the train, one could see the bombed-out buildings. Vienna, once a leading cosmopolitan center of Jewish culture and learning was now *Judenfrei*.

On July 8, they stopped and boarded a train with fewer boxcars. The train, which had been traveling for approximately three and a half days in Germany, arrived in Lower Saxony, near Hanover, south of the towns of Bergen and Belsen. It was an area unknown to the passengers.

It was anticipated that this was to be a three-day rest and recuperation stop. For three hundred fifty passengers, it became a six week stay. For the remaining group, Imi included, it became a half year incarceration in a labor/concentration camp. Manny remembers arriving at the train platform and carrying suitcases

for a long trek by foot several kilometers to their barracks destination. Memories become clouded; on another occasion, Manny
says he and the rest of the children were taken to barracks by
truck.

Rifka Glatz recounts the story her four foot nine inch mother,
Irena Moskovitz, told her. Rifka, then known as Veronica, had
contracted chickenpox during the trip. Irena wrapped her child
in a blanket and *schlepped* her in her arms the entire way to their
new residence. Her son, Tibor, was at Irena's side. There was
general anxiety, especially from all the children who all wanted
to know if they had finally arrived.

Six

At Bergen-Belsen, long, one-story wooden barracks with low sloping roofs, and vertical wooden siding, stretched as far as the eye could see. In an area as big as a large town, approximately 700 by 1,700 meters, nearly two hundred buildings of various sizes and uses had been erected in a clearing that had once been woods.

Begun in 1940, Bergen-Belsen was originally maintained as a prisoner-of-war (POW) camp, first for hundreds of Belgian and French prisoners, but after July 1941 it held nearly twenty thousand Russian POWs.

In April 1943, the camp was included in the Nazi concentration camp system, but was primarily used as a holding center, not to house forced laborers. The complex was comprised of a number of camps, and subcamps. The "residence camp," one of the three main areas, along with the "POW camp" and the "prisoner camp," had four subcamps: the "special camp," the "neutrals camp," the "star camp" and the "Hungarian camp."

Manny remembers the arrival of the Kastzner *csoport* (group)at the long, bare platform with a concrete structure, of sorts. Guards carrying whips hurried them to their destination. Walking four to five abreast, it took over two hours to make a final arduous trek of seven kilometers from the train platform to the barricks.

It seemed as if infinitely more time had elapsed. One of the infamous *Arbeit Macht Frei* signs, a fixture in Nazi Concentration camps, greeted them. What would turn out to be their "residence" for six months contained barbed wire—Manny is sure they were not electrified—fences, searchlights, and towers to make sure there was no mixing of nationalities within the camp. Hungarian guards were in German uniforms, some holding onto tightly leashed dogs. There also were German soldiers (*Wehrmacht* guards & 2nd echelon SS men), carrying machine guns.

Manny knew it was serious. "The feeling was indescribable. Uniforms and helmets did not represent kindergarten. Guns shoot and you die!"

They were told right off what the rules were, not to do this or that. Imi was told not to run; while there, no one—so far as he knew—was ever shot.

Shortly before their arrival, construction on the Hungarian section of the camp had been completed. It contained two long rows of barracks and four out buildings. Two barbed wire fences, five meters apart and likely mined between them, watch towers one hundred meters apart—manned by guards with binoculars and guns—and searchlights from dusk until dawn, discouraged any thoughts of escape. Once inside the *Ungarnlager* (Hungarian camp), they lined up in a heavy rain for roll call *(appell)*; starting at 8:00 PM., it took over two hours. The rains continued for much of July creating much muck and mud. The Kasztner group consisted of 972 women, and 712 men, including 252 children; the oldest man, 82, the youngest child, days old. Amongst them were thirty-five physicians.

Before moving into their barracks, each inmate was given a single (one account say they were provided with two) rough and scraggly blanket—perhaps made out of human hair—a wooden bowl and a spoon. Men were separated from women; they would be together during the day.

According to Manny, they lived "in the elongated barracks, in groups of fifty, sixty, perhaps as many as seventy detainees." One source, however, says there were 130-160 people in each room; this seems more accurate.

Open rafters with angle bracing, also of wood, supported the roofs. The two wooden huts had concrete floors and were divided into eight large rooms. A contingent from a Polish Special Camp occupied three rooms in Building No. 10. Tiny windows allowed sparse sunlight to enter the dismal environs, which were dark, often cold, and smelled. A single toilet, for use at night, was in the rear of each building. Toilet paper was sparse; as a substitute, pages were ripped out of books.

Imi was with Ella, and a group that was made up of females and children. There was another woman in charge. Three-tiered bunks were aligned in blocks of four with narrow aisles between them. Ella, Ivan, now four, and eight-year-old Imi slept on a corner bunk, a narrow bed on a platform. Each bed had a straw mattress covered with the "wool" blanket—bedbugs, fleas and lice.

The following morning, milk and rice pudding was provided for the babies, and youngsters; everyone else had black gruel, a thin cattle turnip soup.

Manny remembered: "We didn't wear camp uniforms [they had their own clothes], but some of us still wore the Star of David on our clothing; some had chanced to take it off during the arduous train ride." It was not required.

Men, women and family latrines were separated. Manny recalls using the men's latrine, which was in a separate barrack, sixty meters away. Invariably, long queues lined up for their turn. The water closets (grimy cesspits full of black flies) consisted of a series of adjacent semi-circular holes cut into raised wooden planks. Bare light bulbs shed little light.

One day, a woman sat there crying; her eyeglasses had fallen into the stinking shit beneath her. She never recovered her precious spectacles.

One of the barracks was the facility for wash-up, a long basin fed by an exposed pipe with only cold water. Periodic hot showers were provided outside the compound in large shower stalls.

"We were marched to the showers." It was only later that Manny and the rest learned that in the "death camps," water was replaced by Zyklon B pellets and the deadly gas they produced.

Manny remembers that the constant concern for survival permeated all activities. "Perhaps the most significant had to do with food. The set of barracks, situated on one side of the main road, was almost directly across from one of the several kitchens. In the morning, depending on what time the roll call took place, men from the compound were permitted to cross the street under guard to bring back rations.

"A significant character of the food was that it was hot. That which passed for coffee, a dark, bitter substance, was hot and the heat was maintained by wrapping the containers in blankets for much of the day. With the coffee was bread which tasted like sawdust but was edible. In the afternoon, similar vats of hot liquid were delivered and at that time 'things' floated; perhaps they were a piece of vegetable or potato or even something like meat, most likely of the equine variety."

"The creativity in converting the material to palatable food was an achievement of remarkable invention. My mother had packed food items when leaving Budapest. Having little information about the prospects of the future, sanitized and refilled tin cans were packed and preserved with a sealing process. She also packed a liter of honey, a liter jar of chicken fat and a slab of fatback/bacon which was never before found in our Kosher home. However, the unknown generates decisions that are out of the ordinary.

"Mother separated the vegetables from the camp's soup. A chopped salad of sorts was then mixed with fat and spread on razor-thin bread. This became several open-face sandwiches, enlarging the meal and satisfying the hungry stomach. The ingredients lasted for the duration of our time in Bergen-Belsen." For a young boy it seemed magical.

"Assembly took place at dawn, followed by roll call at some indeterminate point every morning where a census was taken; this sometimes took two to three hour standing in the sludge. Regardless of the weather, they were counted again and again. Often SS officers showed up accompanied by guard dogs."

The roll call was a daily chore that brought much distress. The instructions were to be lined up outside the barracks at dawn with the inspectors coming at some undefined later time.

At times, their arrival was around ten or eleven in the morning. The exhausting wait was draining. After several weeks of this ordeal, the group's leadership was told that the procedure would be made more orderly. Inspections would begin at 8:00 AM. sharp and everyone must be lined up by that time.

Even in this environment there was, on occasion, a sense of humanity exhibited. A German officer saw a woman standing in what had been shoes before they rotted away because they never dried. Next day he brought her a pair of shoes in a paper bag. Unfortunately, they were much too small.

Kasztner's father-in-law, Jozsef Fischer, was elected camp leader; he helped run the daily activities. Concerted efforts were made to normalize life beyond mere survival. A synagogue was established. The emptied tin cans of food brought for the journey were converted into jewelry items that could be traded for services. A sophisticated list of goods for services was developed. Cigarettes would be exchanged for a haircut, for example, and "prices" were available for most everything. Buyers and sellers negotiated, bargained and sometimes argued. It was a little reminiscent of the world back home, disguising the reality of the life in camp.

Every day, Imi and the others would see people marching past the camp. "They didn't look very happy; some carried farming tools. They didn't look like skeletons, but their heads were shaved; they had deep-set eyes, and prison-like uniforms. "

The Nazis saw fit to excuse the Kasztner group from labor because of their fear that living conditions and work related stress would kill the most vulnerable, thus reducing the number of inmates that could be used as bargaining chips. D-Day had taken place in early June before arrival of the group at Bergen-Belsen, and it was clear to many Nazis, Eichmann and Himmler included, that the war was not going well for Germany.

Endless hours and days had to be filled. The *Chalutz* (Pioneer) youth group organized a small school where they taught Hebrew and French, and even held outdoor gymnastic training. A few of these *Chalutzim* even managed to acquire some alcohol, sometimes getting drunk in their bunks. Most still hoped Palestine would be their eventual destination. Some women conducted exercise classes. Professors of philosophy, psychology, history and political science conducted lectures. Shaul Ladany has a vague memory of Ella trying to "occupy/teach us."

People made an effort to establish some sense of normalcy; everyone seem to be involved in some sort of activity. Chairs, benches and tables were sometimes scattered in the yard as businesses were established.

A typical day for the children consisted of food and school. Manny doesn't remember any playtime at all; "It was mostly boredom," he says. Actually, his peers (and probably Manny) played volleyball, performed gymnastics, and engaged in folk dancing. Everyone wrote letters; the women sewed and washed clothes. If someone was sick, they were allowed to remain in the barracks.

The Hungarian camp was shaped with a slight dogleg at its rear. A forest of evergreens was in the back of the camp, two hundred yards away. The Poles were to the left, on the northwest side in an adjacent, screened-off compound; contact with this and other groups was forbidden. . The rear was vacant, and the front had a road parallel to the encampment. The men and women's latrines were towards the rear, in the back of the camp.

Despite Ella's warning, sometimes Imi ventured too near the barbed-wire fence.

An area where the German soldiers lived had a utility chimney—there was also a crematorium for getting rid of the dead.

There was no hot water; in the morning they washed with cold water. Despite people's best effort, everyone's hair and clothing were full of lice.

"Mother tried to keep herself physically clean." Ella also checked Imi and Ivan throughout the day.

The only time anyone left the Hungarian compound was to go to the periodic hot showers (to the right, just across the road), or go to the hospital, five hundred meters to the northwest from the front entrance. German soldiers supervised the women's showers, often with lewd laughter. Men also left the compound to pick up food and lugged fifty-gallon gasoline vats of a black liquid the Germans called coffee from the camp kitchen.

The Kasztner group usually ate in their barracks. People began to use up their own stocks of foodstuffs. Water and three hundred grams of bread a day were provided. "Even a European peasant couldn't make bad bread," Manny reflected.

Still, as the weeks went by, people became emaciated and were less strong. By the first of August hunger began to set in; some people became faint.

Day-to-day contact was made with the guards. Manny recalls a tall, unpleasant German soldier with black, shiny boots. Herr Fritz said, a sneer in his voice: "I'm boss and you're nothing."

Some of the German soldiers were local. One, they nicknamed "Popeye" after the cartoon character (he always had a pipe stuck in the corner of his mouth).

"He used to open the door to the barracks every day, and shout out, 'Ist alles in ordnung?' (Is everything in order?). He'd wait for an answer, and would then mutter to himself: 'Alles ist ordnung.' (All is in order.) Then he'd move on."

Nevertheless, it was a restricting time; everyone was aware that there was danger.

"At first, in the early days of summer, it had been pleasant but when winter came the rain and snow assailed us; everyone got and remained wet."

His new ankle boots were ruined by standing in the constant water and mud. The wooden dowels, used to reinforce the stitching fell out and the thick soles separated.

"A cobbler my uncle knew had brought tools with him. Don't ask me why or how but he took his tools with him, at least enough to be able to fix a pair of shoes." Cigarettes were traded for the repair. "He used match sticks, thick match sticks, to knock into the shoes so they would stay together. My uncle said, 'Well, I got your shoes fixed. Now stop running around.'"

According to Ladislaus Loeb, (a fellow survivor, aged eleven, at Bergen-Belsen) in his book, *Dealing With Satan*, "on November 22, the Red Cross delivered sixty cases of food, medicines and vitamins. They were given "Star Kosan," which consisted of chocolate powder that included vitamins and other nutrients.

It was consumed with spoons, plied on bread and butter, with water, with jam, and sometimes mixed with glucose."

As winter settled in, Imi contracted double pneumonia; there was a suspicion that he may also have had some TB in his left lung. Many physicians were part of the group but no medication was available for a bacterial disease such as pneumonia. Ella was concerned that if Imi were to be taken to the camp hospital, he may never come back. Palliative measures were designed with the use of mustard powder mixed with water saturating a burlap material that was placed on his chest. This would create a warmth to ease the pain from the disease. Eventually, Imi recovered.

Years later, Jack Shapiro, a physician and long-time friend, discovered a scar on Manny's lungs and confirmed that this might very well be the result of TB. Over the years, it was watched but has remained unchanged

Julie Spiegel was sick in bed much of the time. She contracted measles "and I don't know what else. . . my father continually begged for and got medicines for me."

Negotiations continued with Kasztner in Hungary. On August 18, three hundred eighteen of the "train" Jews, the "special ransomed detail," left Bergen-Belsen; two days later, they arrived in Bregnez and then went on to St. Gallen, Switzerland the next day. No one from the Kasztner family was allowed on this train; only those who could not be conscripted into the war and return to fight the Germans were with this group of "exchange Jews." Imi and his family were not among them. No further contact was made with those people but it was now assumed that the remaining prisoners from the Kasztner group would also be going to Switzerland.

Finally, more than three months later, Kasztner traveled to Germany with SS Standartenfuehrer Becher, to whom he had given additional money to seal the deal. On December 7, after the exchange, the remaining 1,368 "train people" were marched out of Bergen-Belsen, five abreast once again. Small children, the old, the sick and heavy baggage were taken by truck. It took them two to three hours to make the return trip to the Bergen-Hohne platform. By then it was 1:00 AM. All the way, shouting guards and barking dogs harassed them.

Before being put on a German troop passenger train, they waited for another five to six hours in the pouring rain, which repeatedly stopped and started again. All the while they were serenaded by air raid sirens.

This second group, including Imi, Ella, Dezso and Ivan, had come oh-so-close to being included in Bergen-Belsen's final four months of Nazi neglect, leading to mass starvation, disease and death.

By December 1944, the number of prisoners at Bergen-Belsen had increased to around 15,000 from 7,300 in July. In the early months of 1945, the number had grown to 22,000.

As the Allies closed in on Germany, the Nazis began evacuating the remaining prisoners from their camps in the east. By the time of liberation, the camp population had exploded to over 60,000. Conditions continued to deteriorate. Food rations shrank,

Bergen-Belsen

then disappeared. Fresh water was also scarce. Sanitation practically disappeared, and with the overcrowded conditions, and the lack of basic necessities, diseases such as typhus, tuberculosis, and dysentery broke out.

After their arrest in Amsterdam, Anne Frank, sixteen, and her sister, Margot, nineteen, were sent to Auschwitz and then relocated to Bergen Belsen not far from Manny's compound. Thus Imi and Anne Frank breathed the same putrid air and watched thousands of allied aircraft blackening the sky on their way to bring the war to "more essential" targets. Anne Frank and Imi Mandel never met, but Manny has always felt a connection: "She was there. I was there. We were in the same place at the same time. I feel a certain sense of kinship to that."

Three months after Imi's departure, Anne and her sister died of typhus in Bergen-Belsen's "tent camp." One month later, on April 15, 1945 the British liberated the camp, which had become a place for the dead and "the living dead."

The images of the British forced to use bulldozers to push all the dead bodies into a huge mass graves stun us, even today.

Heroic efforts to feed the survivors was counterproductive. Debilitated digestive systems could not accommodate much food. It wasn't until May 11th that the daily death rate fell below one-hundred. During the following two months, the Holocaust claimed an additional 13,944 additional victims from Bergen-Belsen.

Menachem Z. Rosensaft, born in 1948 to two survivors in the Displaced Persons (DP) camp set up at Bergen-Belsen, quotes his mother:

"There was no ecstasy, no joy at our liberation. We had lost our families, our homes. We had no place to go, nobody to hug, nobody who was waiting for us, anywhere. We had been liberated from death and from fear of death, but we were not free from the fear of life."

Through luck, or the persistence of Kasztner, or the actions of some in the about-to-be defeated German High Command trying to gain points from the Allies before surrendering, or perhaps a combination of all of the above, Imi and the other Jews on the Kasztner train bound for Switzerland were able to avoid the terrible fate of those left behind in Bergen-Belsen.

Seven

From the time the "train group" left for Bergen-Belsen on June 30 1944, to the time they left for Switzerland on December 7, much had happened in a world at war now crushing in on the heartland of Europe:

In Budapest, Hungarian authorities ordered the Jews into more than two thousand designated buildings scattered throughout the city. Each building was marked with a Star of David.

At least twenty-five thousand Jews were rounded up and transported to Auschwitz-Birkenau. News of the extent of deportations of Hungarian Jews to the extermination camp provided by eyewitnesses was telegraphed from Switzerland to London and Washington. This led to protests, not only from Britain and the United States, but also from the Pope, the International Red Cross, and King Gustav of Sweden, who sent a plea to Horthy: "Having received word of the extraordinary harsh methods your government has applied against the Jewish population of Hungary, I permit myself to turn to Your Highness personally, to beg in the name of humanity, that you take measures to save those who still remain to be saved of the unfortunate people. This plea has been evoked by my long-standing feelings of friendship for your country and my sincere concern for Hungary's good name and reputation in the community of nations."

Horthy did not answer at first, but eventually wrote back to the Swedish king: "I have received the telegraphic appeal sent me by Your Majesty. With feelings of the deepest understanding, I ask Your Majesty to be persuaded that I am doing everything that, in the present situation, lies in my power to ensure that the principles of humanity and justice are respected. I esteem to a high degree the feelings of friendship for my country that animate[s] Your Majesty and I ask that Your Majesty preserve these feelings toward the Hungarian people in these times of severe trial."

The War Refugee Board's representative in Switzerland, Roswell McClelland, proposed that the Allies bomb the railway lines from Hungary to Auschwitz. The United States military, backed up by the often anti-Semitic State Department, turned a blind eye to the immediacy of the plight of the Jews; industrial targets were deemed more essential, insisting that winning the war as rapidly as possible was the best way to bring an end to the rapidly accelerating Holocaust.

Eichmann met with Rudolf Franz Hoess, Commandant of the concentration camp at Auschwitz. They talked specifically about the percentage of Hungarian Jews that would be physically strong enough for labor. Hoess estimated that between 20 and 25 percent of Hungarian Jews could fit the bill. All Jews who were considered unsuitable for labor would be eliminated. Of the 130,000 Hungarian Jews recruited into labor battalions, approximately 50,000 died from starvation, typhus—or shooting. However, Anna Porter, in her book, *Kastner's Train*, says: "Of the fifty-thousand men in labor battalions only seven thousand survived." Quite a discrepancy. The Russians seized 30,000 prisoners, 20,000 were deported to Germany; the remaining 30,000 stayed behind in Hungary.

In July, Hungarian authorities suspended Jewish deportations, sparing the remaining Jews of Budapest (who were virtually the only Jews remaining in Hungary)—for the present. Just as Eichmann was about to commence deportations of Budapest's Jews, Horthy ordered them to come to an end. Sometime in August, the German's finally submitted to Horthy's pressure; Dome Sztojay was removed as prime minister; he was replaced by General Geza Lakatos.

Despite this, Eichmann hoodwinked the Hungarian authorities and sent another train to Auschwitz; it was filled with prisoners from the Kistarcsa Concentration Camp. Soon after this, another deportation from the concentration camp at Savar took place. Under mounting Nazi pressure, Horthy allowed the deportations to continue. He met with the Nazi Foreign Minister Ribbentrop, who agreed to lessen German interference in Hungarian internal affairs. But at the same time, Horthy was coerced into declaring that the Hungarian army would continue to fight alongside the Germans. Unwilling to open Hungary's borders to the Soviet armies, Horthy still hoped to be able to stop the Russians until the western Allies could occupy his hapless nation.

Eventually Eichmann left Budapest for Germany. He reported to Himmler on the number of Jews killed to date; he estimated the sum total at six million. Of these, four million had been killed in the camps and Ghettos in the East, while another two million died by gunfire—mainly eliminated by the *Eizengruppen* of the SIPO and the SD during the Eastern campaign.

Thirty-two-year old Swedish diplomat, Raoul Wallenberg arrived in Budapest from Sweden on July 9. He carried a list of six hundred thirty Jews for whom Swedish visas had been granted. He carried two knapsacks, which contained a sleeping bag, a windbreaker, and a revolver ("for courage") and a slew of money—filtered through the American Refugee Board—for providing "safe houses" for the Jews (where pass holders could live, protected by the Swedish government), for food for thousands (many had survived on dead horsemeat found in the streets), and for bribing whomever could be bribed. In the capacity of Secretary of the Swedish Legation in Budapest, he was more instrumental than all the allies collectively in saving Hungarian Jews. He extended Sweden's protection to thousands of Jews, thereby delaying their likely transit to Auschwitz.

Count Claus von Stauffenberg was summoned to a conference at Hitler's "Wolf's Lair" in East Prussia. On the 20th of July, he placed a suitcase containing a bomb in hopes of assassinating the Fuehrer. Hitler survived. Stauffenberg didn't; he was soon captured and killed along with hundreds of other suspected co-conspirators. Many in the German hierarchy, including Himmler, were said to be aware of the assassination plot, but didn't know when or where it would occur.

Throughout August, the Russians continued to push the Germans back in the Ukraine, rapidly approaching the region where Lajos's labor battalion was currently working; they had previously been in Vac, Hungary, but were sent wherever their services were required.

In August, Anne Frank and the rest of her family were discovered in their concealed quarters during a hunt for hidden Jews in Amsterdam. Anne and her older sister, Magda, were sent first to Auschwitz and then to Bergen-Belsen.

Monsignor Angelo Roncalli informed Ira Hirschmann (assigned to the U.S. Embassy in Ankara, Turkey) that he had completed sending thousands of baptismal certificates to the Papal

Nuncio in Budapest. Within months, thousands of Jews had been baptized in the air raid shelters of Budapest. Thanks to the immigration certificates forwarded by Monsignor Roncalli, some escaped to Palestine, while others survived because of "safe conduct" passes issued by the Nuncio.

King Michael of Romania ceded Bessarabia and Bukovina (both formerly Romanian territory) to the Soviets. In return Romania received Transylvania, which had previously been a southeastern province of Hungary. The Hungarian police were forced to beat back a demonstration in support of German Nazism. Romania capitulated to the Allies.

As autumn approached, most German leaders realized they were losing the war, and many of the higher-ups began to make plans for jumping ship, or at least laying the groundwork for their survival when the war would come to an end. Himmler directed that all deportations from Budapest and all executions of Jews should cease. Eichmann refused to stop the deportations until he received written orders from his mentor. The Germans cancelled the scheduled deportation of the remaining Jewish population in Budapest. He issued instructions to dynamite all of Auschwitz's gas chambers and crematoria. And he saw to it that the terms of the train negotiations with Kasztner were fulfilled.

Horthy had sought to dissolve the German-Hungarian alliance and was known to have appealed to the Allies for an armistice. While the Russian armies were smashing through Romania toward Hungary, Horthy made a nationwide broadcast, confirming that he had signed an armistice with the Soviet Union. Under its terms his government was declaring war on Germany. Of course this did not sit well with the Germans. They orchestrated a coup and in October, Horth fell from power.

Instead the Germans installed a new Hungarian government dominated by the extremely nationalistic, agriculturally oriented, and very pro-Catholic, anti-Capitalist, anti-Communist, militantly anti-Semitic, fascist *Nyilas* (Arrow Cross) party. Their crossed arrows were a symbol of the Magyar tribes that settled in Hungary, which represented the racial purity of their Hungarian forefathers. The Arrow Cross crushed all resistance, and completed their coup. In mid-October, the Nyilas gangs massacred several hundred Jews in the Yellow Star houses and labor service units.

After Horthy's fall and the coup, Eichmann returned to Budapest. He told Kasztner: "I am back again. You forgot Hungary is still in the shadow of the Reich. My arms are long and can reach the Jews of Budapest as well. The Jews of Budapest will be driven out on foot this time." On October 20, the authorities began systematically emptying the Jewish houses of all their male residents between the ages of sixteen and sixty.

The Soviet army, led by Marshal Rodion Malinovsky, was standing at the gates of Budapest. The Hungarians concentrated more than seventy thousand Jews—men, women, and children—in the Ujlaki brickyards in Obuda, and from there forced them to march on foot to camps in Austria, a 125 mile (200km) journey. Thousands were shot and thousands more died as the result of starvation and exposure to the bitter cold. All told, over ten thousand people died.

On November 15, the Hungarian authorities agreed to the establishment of an international "closed" ghetto in Budapest consisting of seventy-two buildings assigned to house Jews under Swiss protection. This was the so-called "Little Ghetto." At the same time, under the jurisdiction of the authorities, they established the "Big Ghetto" or "General Ghetto." Eventually, the "Big Ghetto" was closed off from the city.

Hannah Szenes was brought before a military court in Budapest on October 28. Less than two weeks later, she was executed.

"As November drew to an end, as the Russians performed their attacks from east to west, so the labor camp people were used to help throw material into the trains that were going westward—" Yehudah Mandel remembered during an interview with the U.S. Holocaust Memorial Museum. "We were always on the move. We were being pushed back to my birthplace."

Lajos got wind that the Nazis, in retribution for some transgression, were about to shoot every tenth man in his battalion. With a few others, in September or October, they broke away from their labor battalion in the Ukraine and made their way back home to Budapest. "I heard that there was an organization that takes Jews in the direction of Vilna, but that whoever couldn't walk would be shot. It took us ten to fourteen days, walking mainly at nighttime, to return to Budapest."

On November 17, as they walked into the city, they agreed: "There is redemption in Budapest." Yehudah realized, "Budapest was about to be encircled. Its fall was expected any day, any hour. I didn't know where my family was. I didn't know there was a ghetto in Budapest." The Germans were prepared to put everyone in a ghetto.

"I found out that the place where we lived was part of the ghetto. My reaction when I entered the area two blocks from our apartment—I realized I was taking my life in my hands. It was snowing. By machinations I got to the place where our apartment was. We lived on the top floor. When I arrived inside, I found some people living in our apartment. There was no roof, and snow was falling onto our Persian rugs. Some pictures had been knocked off the walls, our Rosenthal dishes were broken on the floor—a bomb had hit it. If I didn't get a heart attack, it was because of the grace of God."

In December, Lajos went to the Jewish Community Council. At a Protective House, a friend, a Mr. Hershkowitz, told him that his family was with the Kasztner group. Lajos figured Dezso probably had something to do with their inclusion. At first he thought they might have gone straight to Palestine, or perhaps, God forbid, even to Auschwitz.

Looking up Kasztner, Lajos wanted to know exactly where his family was now; at first Kasztner wouldn't see him, and finally, much to Kasztner's chagrin, Lajos walked past Kasztner's secretary, and burst into his office.

Yehudah once said to his grandson, David, "I was prepared to take a chair and break it over his head."

"Where are they?" shouted Lajos. "Are they alive?" Kasztner told him they were alive, and were presently in Bergen-Belsen.

"Because of my brother, David (Dezso), I had become very active in Zionist work." Residing in a house protected by the Swiss consulate, Lajos became a messenger between safe houses.

"I was young. My face was full. I looked like a real peasant. I would pose as a non-Jew who had been on the front, and had come back because I had been hurt. I was given papers as a *goy*, here on rehabilitation. There were no more streetcars, so I walked.

"We had papers—false papers—the Swedish Schutz-passes (a stupendous fake that saved thousands of lives) had already started. The Nazis accepted these Schutz-passes. I went to Raoul Wallenberg's office to get the Schutz-passes. Posing as a Hungarian soldier, I could walk on the street freely and take the passes to wherever they could be used.

"I met Wallenberg many times, but I didn't get to talk with him for five minutes. He spoke German. He would say: 'Give him whatever her needs, fast, because he has to go.' My sadness is that I never got to sit down and talk with this angelic man.

"They [Wallenberg's people] were offered offices at the consulate. They did the best they could—the false documents, the uniforms, guns, etc. They held [clandestine] meetings somewhere else [other than at the consulate].

"I was never in the ghetto. I was in the protected house. I got dressed and tried to leave the protected houses to go to the Swedish consulate in Buda. I never remember having to wait. No one stopped me when I left the consulate. Sometimes I met Nazis and pretended I was with them. 'Those Jews!' I said.

"Many times I did other things. We had to free these, mostly young, strong, Jews before they were shot and thrown in the Danube. We got the command to free the people in the Tolens House [Manny is unfamiliar with this place]. The commander dressed up as a Lieutenant. We went to concentration prisons wearing Hungarian gendarme uniforms. We showed our false papers. Using them, we would take fifty to sixty Jews out. We said, we will do the right thing, and will take care of them. Just give them to us." All told, he participated in rescuing three hundred Jews from the prison.

"The streets of Budapest were completely empty—people were scared. Very rarely did you see a car. Most of the vehicles had been taken by the military. Bombing was going on. We marched the people back to different places—to non ghettos, protected by gates. We said don't worry, you will be safe. We will take you where you should be. They realized they were in safe hands.

"Getting away from camp was risky; any second I might be shot by Hungarian Nazis. If they shot a Jew, they would get a thank you. We runners kept on the same clothes and shoes; some of us had shoes with no soles.

"I was part of the Zionist underground. We had to bring in paper. We didn't have water, so I went into a cellar with a dish to gather water to make soup, or to bring to a sick person. We gathered bread and cheese. Many people did the same thing.

"The winter of '44 was terribly cold. We who had been in the Ukraine could stand it. There, sometimes we slept in the snow wearing a coat—the snow kept us warm."

Eichmann was recalled to Germany in December. Meanwhile, at Bergen-Belsen, now redesignated as a concentration camp; SS Hauptsturmfuhrer Josef Kramer, previously at Auschwitz-Birkenau, became the new camp commander. He had inherited 15,257 inmates. Some survived.

During December and January 1945, the *Nyilas* took as many as twenty thousand Jews from the ghetto, shot them on the banks of the Danube and threw their bodies into the river.

Eight

Imi, Ella, Dezso and Ivan sat together while a weather-beaten German troop transport made its way southward from Ber- gen- Belsen, across the ravaged German countryside. Freedom for the 1,368 Hungarian Jews was still more than eight hundred miles away in neutral Switzerland.

Manny remembers seeing Russian and American planes, and bombed-out bridges. A frigid nip in the air heralded the impending winter. The third-class cars were not sealed; many of the windows were broken. Everyone stuffed themselves with sugar, margarine and bread. Diarrhea, accompanied with vomiting, was the inevitable result. The corridors and toilets reeked.

By war's end, between 26,000 and 27,000 Jews would reach Switzerland, escaping persecution by the Nazis. Another 25,000 Jewish civilian refugees were refused entry; one Swiss official was heard to say: "Our little lifeboat is full."

The trip to Switzerland took three "slow" days (December 4th through the 7th). On the sixth of December they reached

Ivan Fleischmann, (left) and Imi, 1945. Shortly after leaving Bergen-Belsen.

Lindau. While stopped briefly at a station in Lustenau, Austria, Kasztner met the train, where he was greeted with smiles and much applause. Kasztner then returned to Germany and on to Budapest while the train continued its journey towards the Swiss border.

The train left Lustenau at seven that evening. By midnight, they crossed the Rhine where it flows into Lake Constance, which separates Germany from the northeastern part of Switzerland. At 1:00 AM they reached Sankt Margarethen, just inside Switzerland, where they debarked and changed trains. The Swiss trains purposely have a different narrower gauge from their neighboring countries—Germany, France, Italy, Austria and Liechtenstein— so no one could invade by rail.

Though Switzerland has a long history of remaining neutral, and managed to stay out of hostilities; after the surrender of France in 1940, she found herself completely surrounded by a German vice. Switzerland's leaders had opted for appeasement, but tougher individuals made it perfectly clear to the Third Reich that the cost of an invasion would be extreme.

Switzerland has a multicultural heritage; it is multilingual, with four national languages: German, French, Italian and Romanish. The train was headed to the German region.

After boarding the Swiss train, the first thing the Hungarian Jews did, amidst cheers of tearful joy and a mounting sense of relief, was applaud when an individual, in a symbolic gesture, ripped off his Yellow Star of David he had kept as a souvenir.

It was a cold December night as they marched along St. Galen Street to the barracks that had been prepared for them. Friendly Swiss soldiers, members of the Women's Auxiliary Corps and Red Cross personnel met them. The newly liberated group's initial destination was an army barracks, a large heated gymnasium where they were fumigated, deloused and decontaminated. The Swiss, noted for being very fastidious, operated with strict rules.

After basking in hot showers, they were given brand new warm clothes. Toys were handed out to the children. Fingerprints and photographs (with numbers strung around their

Imi, Ivan and Ella. Heiden, Switzerland, 1945.

necks) were the next order of business. Afterwards, they had the opportunity to stretch out and relax comfortably on mattresses that had no bedbugs, lice or fleas.

Imi and Ivan's ribs were showing. For them and almost everyone else, food had become a serious concern. Arriving for a meal, the survivors couldn't believe their eyes—tables had been set up with fresh tablecloths, shiny plates, cutlery and crystal glasses. They were served cheese, soup, potatoes and bread. Had they forgotten their manners? Some had.

After four days of becoming integrated back into a peaceful, comfortable, food-enriched environment, sans filth, smells, armed guards, barbed wire, ill health and anxiety, they were taken by another train to St. Gallen. The train continued to the French part of Switzerland, in Caux, near Montreux overlooking the Alps with a comanding view of Lake Geneva. It had become a transitional point for displaced persons.

The non-religious majority stayed at the Caux Palace—then known as Hotel Esplanade—at one time the largest and most luxurious hotel in Switzerland; it catered to the "royalty of Eu-

Switzerland, 1945. Imi at far right.

rope." The *Belle Époque* building, designed by local Swiss architect, Eugene Jost, is known for its many turrets and towers, its ballrooms and chandeliered lobby.

In May 1944, the resort hotel had been taken over by the Red Cross, requisitioned for civilian internees, and later for escaped Allied prisoners of war. The rooms were heated. They had baths, and a sense of privacy. Shorn of lice and bedbugs, the Hungarian group remained in luxury for two to three weeks, and were fed "lots of potatoes" and chocolates. The Red Cross gave more toys to the youngsters.

The refugees were no longer bound by the strict restrictions of the concentration camp—it was a complete contrast to the strict regimentation they had experienced in Bergen-Belsen. This was a time to unwind mind, body and soul. Ella, now thirty seven, went skiing with her now eight-year-old son. Lajos' sister, Helen, had sent Imi a pair of shoes from Philadelphia, which he used as skis. He and his mother also went sledding; Ella borrowed a Flexible Flyer type of sled, which they rode one time down the hill seven hundred meters from Caux to Montreux. They walked back up the hill.

Time was limited in this wonderland; everyone had to be dispersed from Caux to make room for other group arrivals. At the time, the World Zionist Congress was making arrangements for those who wanted to go to Palestine.

Twenty children, including Imi, were sent with Ella to a boarding school in Heiden; it was functioning as a home for displaced children. Paul Mueller was the Director. After the war, he immigrated to America and ran a children's home in Philadelphia.

Gabriella, whom everyone now called Ella, was sent with the group of children, ages six to fourteen, to be a teacher, caretaker and translator. She had been an elementary school teacher in Yugoslavia and could speak Hungarian with the children, French and German with the rest of the staff. Having his mother as the teacher caused Imi some problems with his peers. When anyone got caught breaking a rule, they thought Imi was the tattletale. Manny recalls sometimes he was even "beaten up" over it.

Cantor Moshe Neu, a colleague of Lajos—they had been students in Vienna—was currently living in Zurich. He was reached by Lajos and was able to arrange for Ella to get in touch with her husband.

The Mandels were able to reestablish contact, and began to correspond by mail and telegraph. There were no working telephones in Budapest, about to be overrun by the Russian Army. For the present, they agreed to stay where they were. Ella and Imi and Ivan would remain in Heiden.

Ella had other ideas. She refused to ever set foot in Hungary again. She planned to immigrate to Palestine and urged Lajos to join them. Other members of the group were also making plans. Some stayed in Switzerland; others went back to Hungary. Lajos contacted his sister Helen who sent Ella a CARE package from Philadelphia to tide her over until she was settled. They remained in Heiden from February to August 1945, three months after the war in Europe was over. Once again, Lajos reached out to Ella but could not change her mind. She wrote again that she never would return to Hungary. She was determined to go to Palestine.

The Rumbach Synagogue had been used as a hospital and its dome was damaged by bombs. Lajos was instrumental in arranging for the repair of the dome so the Synagogue could function. In fact, there were preparations for him to lead services for the High Holidays, 1945. However, he wanted to reconnect with his family and negotiated a three month leave of absence. While the formal agreement was for a leave of absence, he knew that if he got to Palestine, he had no intention to return. He got in touch with the underground organization, *Breicha*, that arranged for illegal immigrants to reach Palestine.

While preparing to leave Switzerland with Dezso, Imi and Ivan, Ella purchased two watches using money she had been paid for her services as a teacher. She bought an Omega and a Longines, one of which she put on Imi's wrist. She purchased them in the event she needed to barter, if necessary. To this day, Manny still has his watch.

In August of 1945, Imi, Dezso and Ivan boarded a train which took them to Italy. They continued by British troop carriers to Bari on the Adriatic Sea, just above the heel of Italy. The well-known port and university city was named after Saint Nicholas of Bari.

Earlier, Bari had gained the unwelcome distinction of being the only European city to have experienced the effects of chemical warfare. The decision was made by President Roosevelt to stockpile mustard gas bombs in Europe in case the Nazis ever instigated their use. In December 1943, while the secret cargo was still in its hold, a Liberty ship, the SS *John Harvey*, was sunk in the port. A cloud of gas was released over the city, causing hundreds of casualties.

For nearly two weeks the Mandels remained in Bari, one of the largest displaced persons camps in Europe. Here, the conditions were dreadful; water was sorely lacking. Finally they boarded a British troop transport in the coastal city of Taranto in Puglia, which lies between the heel and toe of Italy's southern coast. From this important commercial port and the main Italian naval base, they embarked to Palestine.

Nine

During the weeks that Ella was preparing to depart Switzer-land for Palestine, Budapest was being occupied by Soviet troops. Lajos was hiding out in a crowded basement with other Hungarian Jews and none knew what to expect. Were they trading in one barbarian horde for another?

"We were 'liberated,'" Lajos remembered. "I had tried to keep my people together—the *menschheit* [mankind] of human-ity. A Russian soldier appeared in the cellar of the house where we had been hiding. It was dangerous; the Russians brought all kinds of problems." What would this warrior do? Shoot them? Rape one of the women? "This soldier, a typical Russian peasant, shouted: 'Give me your watch.'" Lajos, like the others, breathed an inward sigh of relief. They gave him their watches. Eventu-ally, "I went back to our own apartment."

Hungary officially surrendered on January 21 1945, but it wasn't until February that all resistance in Budapest was at last quelled. On the eleventh, the Arrow Cross party men finally stopped hunting down Jews that were hiding, as well as those who had been living openly, usually with false papers.

February 14, about three and a half weeks after the surrender, the Soviet troops completed the liberation of Budapest, but
not before the Germans blew up the Danube River bridges. Out
of a total population of 800,000 Jews, likely the second largest in
Europe, over 400,000 had been deported to Auschwitz.

  More than 100,000 still remained in the city. The Russians
discovered 25,000 Jews in the "Little Ghetto," and another 70,000
holed up in the "Big Ghetto." Once the Germans had left, 25,000
more Jews eventually came out of hiding. The unburied bodies
of 10,000 murdered Jews were found amongst the ruins.

  Seeing the Third Reich's dreams tumbling down around
him, Eichmann was heard to say that if matters came to the worst,
he would return to Prague and shoot his family and himself. He
didn't. He escaped the roundup of war criminals and eventually
made his way, like a number of other top and middle echelon
Nazis, to South America, mostly Argentina.

  Lajos' birthday was March 3. "My congregants asked me
what I wanted for my birthday. Of course, most of all, I wanted
to be reunited with my family. Of what use were ordinary possessions now? What would I do with a replacement set of dishes
or having the Persian rugs cleaned? A good meal might have sufficed for the moment, but it was even difficult to find a loaf of
bread."

  He thought for a moment. "I want you to come to the Rumbach Synagogue for a day or two and work as laborers." Everyone knew why he was making such a request. "When the Russians came in, all the dirt from the building's bomb damage and
use as a hospital was there." Every man and woman agreed. "We
rebuilt part of the Temple that was ruined. We had services in the
Temple."

  Himmler was up to his "new" tricks. Between April 6 and

11, three trainloads of prisoners left Bergen-Belsen; they were comprised of prominent Dutch Jews, Hungarian Jews, Jewish prisoners from neutral countries and Jewish prisoners holding foreign passes. He was hoping to make use of these prisoners in his negotiations with the Allies.

One after another, the Allies were discovering the horrors of the Concentration Camps. On the fourth of April, American soldiers stumbled upon Ohrdruf, a subsidiary camp of Buchenwald. A week later, American troops from the 6th Armored Division entered the main camp at Buchenwald. Then, on the fifteenth, British forces liberated Bergen-Belsen; the horror that had become a hellhole four months after the last of the 1,676 Hungarian Jews, members of the Kasztner group, had been transported to Switzerland.

Even after they were freed from Bergen-Belsen, about twelve thousand inmates died from disease, primarily typhus. A large number also died because it took the British medical corps several weeks to design a cuisine that could be digested by prisoners who had not had regular food for too long.

Near the end of April, a remnant of the Luftwaffe bombed Bergen-Belsen hitting one of the hospitals treating the sick; the blasts injured or killed several Red Cross workers. Ironically, the combined Allied air forces couldn't or wouldn't bomb the tracks leading to Auschwitz during the war. Eight days prior to war's end, Hitler had ended his own life in his underground bunker in Berlin. Nearly a month before that, FDR had died of a cerebral hemorrhage in Warm Springs, Georgia.

On May 4, part of the German Army surrendered to the British on the Luneberg Heath where the Bergen-Belsen camp is located. Three days later, the rest of the German Army surrendered to General Eisenhower. By then, the allies knew the full story about what had happened at Auschwitz. Of the Jewish communities of the Soviet Union, Romania and Hungary, only about half remained. There are no precise figures on the number of Jews murdered. Estimates range from 4.5 million to more than six million.

The most active accomplices of the Germans in these acts of extermination were the Ukrainians and Lithuanians, but they also had many helpers among the Croatians, Rumanians, Hungarians and Slovaks. As Tom Lehrer used to sing: "And, everybody hates the Jews."

Le Deluge et Apres le Deluge

In 1944, Rosa, Lajos's mother, was sent to Auschwitz. Ella's parents, Armin and Paula Klein, and her sisters, Magda and Ilona, and Ilona's daughter, Judika (little Judy), were also sent to Auschwitz, as was Dezso's fiancé, and Dushko, Bella and Lilly's son. More than likely, Berta Mandel, Jeno's wife, was deported to Auschwitz. Except for Magda and Ilona, and Dezso's fiancé, every one of them died in the infamous murder factory. Magda and Ilona remarried and lived in Israel.

Sanyi, Magda's husband, Erno, Ilona's husband, Ella's brothers, Jeno and Zsiga, all died in labor camps. These slave labor battalions did heavy work substituting for those men

Imi with paternal grandmother, Budapest 1943.

who were in the military. Many of these worker prisoners, as in the Mandel and Klein families, died under conditions of starvation and overwork. Interestingly, Ella's youngest brother, Sanyi, drafted into the Yugoslav army, was taken POW in Italy, survived typhus and survived the war. Magda's in-laws, Mr. and Mrs. Hajdu, were killed during the Novi Sad *razia*.

Lajos escaped from a labor battalion and was able to make his way to Budapest and later to Palestine. Dezso survived and was reunited with Chava; they married and had twins. Soon after the establishment of the State of Israel, he secured a prestigious teaching position in the Reali School in Haifa. Suddenly, at the age of thirty five, he died. Chava never remarried.

Lajos, Ella and Imi eventually immigrated to America. All of these people, flesh and blood, were from one extended family! It was all a roll of the dice; though there were countless Jew haters in Europe, no one was able to determine exactly "whose number" would come up.

Ten

In September 1945, the British troopship began its journey, sailing from Taranto in Puglia, southeast across the Mediterranean Sea to Egypt. The group of Hungarian Jews, which included Ella, Imi, Ivan and Dezso, debarked in Haifa Harbor in the far northwest quadrant of Palestine.

Looking back, Manny, in a moment of reflection, recalled his state at that time: "Compared to the adults, I had no permanent emotional scarring from the long ordeal we had experienced."

While perhaps it is true that the perspectives of a child make healing easier, the events he had experienced—the Danube *razzia*, fear of the unknown, Bergen-Belsen, deportations, separations, humiliations, bombings, death and destruction, the loss of loved ones, and the loss of a home, surely had some effect on the young boy's psyche.

Lajos was still in Budapest. He had written to Ella but didn't get any answer. His prospects were bright in Budapest; he was in line to become the Secretary General of the Chaplaincy Service. Lajos was in the prime of his career. Having served for ten years, he was in the middle of his twenty-year lifetime contract. He also was the youngest cantor in a major Jewish Community where his reputation was established. He was comfortable in Budapest, having achieved a life and career goal. Then he got a letter from Ella. "She said they were on their way to Israel, then Palestine." Lajos proceeded to formulate his plans to meet his family there. Upon his departure, he would be the Rumbach Synagogue's final *fokantor*.

Kibbutzim (collective farms or settlements) represented the "new Jew." They embodied the principles of hard work and communal sharing. The *kibbutzniks* led vigorous, open-aired lives, usually in well-kept, attractive surroundings—tended lawns, flower gardens, and newly planted trees. Education and the welfare of the young were foremost. Yehudah recalled that life on a kibbutz was very safe. "They feed you. They house you. You have wrap-around security." Ella, with Imi and Ivan, were sent to *Kibbutz Shaar HaAmakim.*

Affiliated with the *Hashomer Hatzair* movement, Ella's kibbutz was made up of pioneers from Hungary and Yugoslavia. Founded in 1933 on the side of gently sloping hills, it would, even in later years, maintain its original leftist orientation.

Dezso went to *Kibbutz Maanit*, established before the war by his training group (*Hachsharah*). His work assignment there was not in education but in heavy labor, mostly operating a pile driver.

Although Dezso's civil marriage to Chava Eisdorfer had taken place in Hungary, they were separated when she was immediately deported to Auschwitz. She survived and they were reunited in Palestine as husband and wife. Dezso, disappointed with some of the philosophy on the kibbutz, contemplated leaving. He found a teaching position in the Reali School in Haifa and found housing in Nesher. By that time, they were parents of twins, born in 1947.

Upon arrival in Palestine, Imi adapted to his new home.

He was now called by his Hebrew name, Zvi, called his mother *Ima*, and referred to his father as *Abba*. Ivan was renamed Joash (a later King of Israel). He and Zvi lived together in the kibbutz but the difference in their ages placed them in separate groups. Joash's mother and father separately made their way out of Hungary. When they arrived in Palestine, they joined their child in the kibbutz. Eventually, they left *Shaar HaAmakim* because Dr. Imre Fleishmann, Joash's father, a veterinarian, established his large animal practice. Today, Joash, a father of four and grandfather of eight, lives in Omer, near Beersheba with his wife, Chava.

On the kibbutz, Ella was assigned to pick onions, carrots and radishes, the vegetables to which she could cause the least damage. This was the lowest rank for a worker. The other cash crops were various fruits; their handling required certain training which Ella lacked. The work was hard for a thirty-eight-year-old woman with no experience in agriculture. Nevertheless, Manny remembers that his mother was pleased with the new challenge.

Zvi, Shaar HaAmakan, 1946.

Zvi and Joash lived with their contemporaries—age groups according to the social system of the kibbutz. A caretaker and a teacher were assigned to each group. Zvi lived with the Oak Group, consisting of twenty children, both boys and girls. The children saw their parents when they came home from work.

In the kibbutz, most of the other children were not Holocaust kids. They arrived with families before 1939 when the war engulfed Europe and many were native born. Zvi didn't speak Hebrew; they did. Everyone ran around barefooted. Zvi didn't have their calloused feet: "It takes years to develop them," Manny explained.

The work organizer of the kibbutz indicated they needed someone in the kitchen. Ella was the elder of the group. She volunteered. Immediately, she improved the food by seasoning it with salt, pepper, and margarine; she prepared real food—dairy, vegetables, and chicken. She ultimately became the chief chef, cooking for 230-240 people. At the time, the *kibbutz* nominated Ella to become a member, which was an honor since she had only been there two to three months, and membership was not usually offered for at least two years.

Zvi was learning Hebrew, a third language and it was not an easy transition. A fourth grader, he lived in a room with three or four children. It was a cinderblock building covered with stucco or plaster, a heated building. With no sisters, Zvi was particularly startled to see a girl and boy, side-by-side when he first went to the showers. "My notion was that boys showered one place, girls another." Zvi made a beeline out of the shower room shouting for a towel. He soon returned, and later became used to it. "It was a delightful adventure." Still, the kibbutz operated within strict guidelines concerning boys and girls.

Lajos was determined to meet his family in Palestine. He joined a group of like-minded Jews from Budapest who desired to find their way there. In preparation for leaving, he boxed up three crates of books, pictures and other items in his apartment to be sent to his future home. The custom-made furniture, the grand piano, the Persian carpets and much of the other household goods accumulated since his 1930 marriage were sold for a sum equivalent to eleven U.S. dollars. This was a significant amount of money in the days of extreme inflation in 1946. The inflation created "millionaires" out of everybody because a loaf of bread or a postage stamp cost millions of pengo, the Hungarian currency.

Italy would be Lajos's initial destination. That is where possibilities existed to find a way to Palestine which would most likely be through illegal means. In order to avoid being noticed, all members of the group pretended to be deaf mutes suffering from shell shock. Most did not speak Serbo-Croatian, the language of Yugoslavia, the country through which they had to travel to Italy.

The ploy was like a macrocosm of Sargent's painting, *Gassed*, depicting an orderly leading a group of soldiers who had been blinded by mustard gas.

Lajos, too, pretended to have lost his hearing. They didn't want to appear as foreigners; this way all of them would be perceived as wounded veterans of the war—Jews were still fair game.

"We were able to navigate successfully through Yugoslavia to Italy," Yehudah recalled. "When we finally reached La Spezia, a fishing village on the west coast of Italy near Pisa, the British made the Italian government arrest us, swelling those incarcerated at La Spezia to a thousand Jews. We were there for nine or ten weeks. During that time, I performed religious services.

"We were determined to leave La Spezia at night." Lajos was on a small illegal immigration vessel, the *Dov Hoz* (named after one of the founders of the Haganah), coming out of La Spezia. In the morning, two British destroyers blocked them. It was a scene reminiscent of the book, *Exodus* and the film of the same name and likely one of its inspirations.

The bestselling novel by Leon Uris, published in 1958, about the founding of the State of Israel begins with a ship, the *Exodus*, being used to transport Jewish refugees, mostly children, from a British detention camp in Cyprus to Palestine. The British blockade the ship to prevent those on board from going ashore. In response, the passengers go on a hunger strike until the authorities relent.

In the actual incident, an antiquated, former American steamship, the *SS President Warfield*, set sail from France with 4,515 refugees on July 11, 1947 flying a banner on its side, "Haganah Ship Exodus 1947."

It was captained by twenty-three-year-old Yitzhak Ahronovitch who was born in Poland but had emigrated to Palestine with his family when he was ten. As soon as *Exodus* left French territorial waters, British naval vessels shadowed the ship.

About twenty kilometers from the coast of Palestine, the *Exodus* was rammed and boarded by British naval officers. Two passengers and one crewman were killed and another thirty injured. The *Exodus* was eventually towed to the port of Haifa where the passengers were forced onto more seaworthy ships heading back to France.

When the ships reached the French shores, the passengers of the *Exodus* refused to exit their ships and with the encouragement of Haganah representatives, went on a hunger strike. The French government refused to forcibly remove the refugees.

Despite protests, the British decided to move the ships to Hamburg, Germany in the British occupation zone. Those on board were then forcibly removed and taken to British detainee camps.

On the La Spezia docks, all one thousand of the stranded

Jews, including Lajos, were defiant. They went on a hunger strike for ninety-eight hours. "There was a great hue and cry," Yehudah recalled.

Herbert Morrison, British Deputy Prime Minister was in Milan at a conference. He was ordered to La Spezia to negotiate the ending of the hunger strike, which was becoming another embarrassment to the British.

Yehudah remembered: "Morrison said we shouldn't have a hunger strike. If we stopped, he would get us permits to go to Israel as legal immigrants. He negotiated an agreement."

The group was provided with a second boat, the *Eliyahu Golomb*, named after an early *Haganah* leader, and were given safe conduct to Haifa, without the usual "detour" to Cypress. The two boats left La Spezia in late summer of 1946.

"When we got to Palestine, since I was a leader on one of our boats, I had to stay aboard until everyone disembarked and everything had been taken off," Yehudah said. "When I went ashore, I discovered that Ella had not seen me so she left. I told a taxi driver that all I had was one English pound. He said, not to worry, he would take me to Shaar HaAmakim free-of-charge." The taxi driver dropped Lajos off at the kibbutz where Ella, Zvi, and Joash were now living.

By the time Lajos arrived, Ella, Zvi and Yoash had been living at Shaar HaAmakim for nearly a year and he had not seen them for the better part of two years, since their deportation from Budapest in 1944.

Zvi was on an overnight excursion when his father arrived at the kibbutz. When Zvi returned, his first instinct was to leap into his father's arms, but he was more restrained, more adult now. Instead he said, "Shalom Abba!"

"Shalom Zvi," his father answered.

An uneasy silence settled over the reunited family. Lajos knew full well what went on in the kibbutz; it was totally non-observant. He looked around, sizing up the situation. To him, Ella lived in a cinderblock hut glossed over with slipshod stucco.

Later, he saw how the kibbutz celebrated the Sabbath and recalled that "Essentially these Zionists transposed it into issues of nature—Moses could talk to animals and God, and religion didn't exist." This was not for Lajos. He knew he could have pursued other musical opportunities there but he wanted to remain in his field. He was professionally and religiously committed as a Hazzan. One thing was clear: he was definitely unwilling to remain in the kibbutz. He was anxious to reestablish his roots in the outside world.

Lajos renewed prior contacts from Europe. He was invited to sing on the Kol Yisrael radio. He davened in Jerusalem and his exceptional talent was soon recognized. He was offered a position in Jeshurun, the largest synagogue in Jerusalem. He tried to secure housing which was enormously expensive and required *dmei mafteach* (key money) which he did not have. He had to turn down the Jeshurun offer because the congregation did not offer any help.

A man named Friedman heard him audition in Jerusalem. He told Lajos that there was a vacancy in his congregation in Haifa at the Carmia Synagogue. That congregation would arrange housing without any key money required.

Meanwhile, Ella and Zvi were happy and had become acclimated to the kibbutz where they had spent the previous year. They became part of a fabric of the society of the kibbutz. However, there was no question that family unity would require their move to Haifa.

In the time period that Lajos was journeying from Budapest to Palestine, some members of the kibbutz thought Ella should begin a regular social life.

Complicating matters, there had been rumors that she, an attractive woman, had formed a "relationship" or that someone from the kibbutz was "interested" in her. What they really meant was that "maybe something should" be going on. Who spread the tale was never known.

Afraid that this would compromise Lajos, Dezso visited the kibbutz and found that there was no reason for concern—it was nothing more than gossip that exists in any society. He talked to Ella about it and she denied it. End of story.

Yehudah said, "I stayed for seventeen days. I lived with Ella in her cabin while at the kibbutz." Manny has never been sure about the exact dates—but he does know that his father was there sometime in August or September.

Lajos, now forty-five and in his prime, accepted a permanent position as a cantor at the Carmia Synagogue. However, it would still be difficult for him to make a decent living there, or for that matter, anywhere else in Palestine. He performed numerous concerts in Pevsner Hall. He also formed a choir. Zvi sang alto with the group.

Lajos found housing in Haifa in a building where a member of the congregation had erected two additional floors. It was a brand new apartment with a large balcony overlooking Haifa Bay. The landlord/owner was a milkman, Mr. Stein, who rose at three in the morning, every day, retrieved his donkey from a barn, bought two large containers of milk and delivered them to the nearby homes, one liter at a time.

The apartment consisted of a day room which doubled as the main bedroom and another bedroom in which Zvi slept. His room doubled as the music room and included a baby grand piano. The kitchen, typical of its time, had cold running water. Two stoves were located on the counter tops, one a Primus for high heat and the other slow heating burners. Both operated on kerosene with that container on a porch outside the kitchen; it had to be replenished periodically. The porch also doubled as a drying area for laundry. An ice box was in a hallway and it had to be restocked about every two days. The WC (water closet) was separate from the bathroom which contained a tub with shower and a sink. To have hot water, the family needed to purchase heating elements that were inserted into a small water heater.

Shopping was conveniently located and was a daily task. A pharmacy, located a long block away, offered the only available telephone.

Zvi enrolled in the fifth grade of the local elementary school. His academic career was inconsistent; he entered the first grade speaking Hungarian in Budapest. He "completed" the second grade in Bergen-Belsen. Third grade occurred in Switzerland and fourth grade, speaking a new language, Hebrew, was completed in the kibbutz. By the fifth grade in Haifa, Zvi's Hebrew was excellent. Before leaving for America, he was a student in the Geula Elementary School through half of grade seven. "We lived in the kibbutz from 1945 through 1946. For the next three years, we lived in Haifa," Manny said.

In November of 1947, the U.N. General Assembly voted in favor of the partition of Palestine into independent Jewish and Arab states with Jerusalem internationalized. At the time, there were 1,220,000 Arabs and 650,000 Jews living in the area, Yehuda, Ella and Zvi, now eleven, among them.

Zvi observed the British leaving and the last High Commissioner, Sir Alan Cunningham, boarding a warship in the Haifa harbor.

Lajos's family had been decimated, with only his youngest brother, David, surviving. And, of course, there was his sister, Helen, who had immigrated to America in 1914.

In February, 1948, Lajos was able to arrange to visit his sister. He sailed to "the land of milk and honey" on the last Russian ship leaving Haifa, the liner, Rossia. He wanted to see his sister, one of the family's few survivors, but also to get a glimpse of America. The family had maintained contact through the years and Aunt Helen sent useful items including a pair of roller states for Zvi who became a very good skater.

Manny describes his Father's reactions to America. He realized early in his visit that none of Europe's World War II scars were evident in this new land. The cantorate was a viable profession. By interesting contrast, Israel did not need cantors. He thought that he could rekindle his dreams if he could resettle in the United States. However, immigration laws did not permit that because his place on the Czechoslovakian quota would require a waiting period of years.

Obscure laws sometimes become useful. In researching immigration laws, Helen's son, Bernie, a senior partner in one of Philadelphia's leading law firms, discovered that clergy were exempt from quota requirements. Nevertheless, cantors, at that time, were not considered clergy. But, Lajos, now referred to as Yehudah, had full qualifications as a rabbi, having earned ordination (*smicha*) from the Yeshiva in Ungvar and the Yeshiva in Pressburg. Now he needed to find a rabbinic position.

Yehudah had established a relationship with the First Romanian American Congregation in New York City. When discussing the immigration issue with the rabbi, Chaim Porille, he was offered a solution. The rabbi proposed that, because of his qualifications, Yehudah should become the associate rabbi. With that certification, his immigration was secured. He was required to leave the country; he went to Canada and re-entered the United States as a non-quota immigrant.

Yehudah's actual position was as the cantor at the Romanian-American Congregation, the "Romanische shul" named *Shaarey Shomayim*. The building stood until 2007. It was located in New York's Lower East side, on Rivington Street, a block from Hester Street, and a block from the Fulton Fish Market. For many years, it served as the "Carnegie Hall" for the cantorate. Most cantors of note in the first half of the twentieth century held positions or appeared there.

When Yehudah Mandel first sang there, the congregation

applauded, something that had never been seen before. Yehudah had no teaching or communal duties, only to *daven* or appear once a month with a professional choir and during the holidays. He commuted from his sister's home in Philadelphia to New York; staying at the Broadway Central, a kosher hotel.

Having secured a position, Yehudah wrote to Ella and asked her to join him in America. It took a year for them to make the arrangements. In the meantime, Israel declared its statehood on May 15, 1948. The United States. was the first to grant full and unconditional recognition to the provisional government of Israel.

As if on cue, the shooting started. "Once again a war ended my piano career. I had started to take lessons at a famous institute in Budapest when the Second World War changed everything. Nearly a decade later, in Haifa, I resumed taking lessons, studying under Reuben Frankel, who had to go with the army when the War of Independence began."

At the time, twelve-year-old Zvi was in the sixth grade at the Geula elementary school. The school was emptied out because it was being used as a training facility; their classes were now held in the Technion. "We had tremendous enthusiasm for our independence, lots of yelling and cheering," Manny remembers.

"To protect against possible air raids, which never happened, we paper taped the windows of our apartment in the fashion we had learned in Europe. Both out enormous porch and our building were splattered with bullet holes, the cement façade pockmarked with stray ammunition. There was an Arab enclave just south of Haifa called Vaadi Rushmiya; the bullets must have come from there. One day, the British-trained English teacher, after being on active duty for some time, returned and announced: 'We will no longer be studying English. We will study American.' Again, we students cheered the announcement as an expression of the intense dislike for the British.

"At the beginning of the war, we were eating Australian imported fish, which became a staple of our cuisine. We had plenty of food because vegetables and dairy were abundant. Only butter was rationed and meat was scarce. Misinterpreting my mother's correspondence, my father thought we might be starving so he airmailed us a package from the US that cost forty five dollars. It contained corn flakes, an unknown breakfast food, and tins of Chicken-of-the-Sea brand tuna. When we received it, I said to myself: 'What kinds of chickens do Americans raise? It's the oiliest chicken I ever had.' My mother was able to prepare fine food from these strange ingredients. Clearly, my English scholarship left much to be desired."

A new adventure was on the horizon, the fifth country in which the family Mandel would live, over a five-year period. Ella and Imi left for America on March 7, 1949.

"We came to a sublet apartment in Greenwich Village," Manny said, "and next settled on East Eleventh Street while I attended parts of seventh and eighth grade at P.S. Number Three."

It was a close knit Jewish community, Yiddish to the core. However, when Ella, who spoke no English, arrived in New York, she was looked down on as a "lesser" person, an "uneducated" Jew, even though she was fluent in Hungarian, German and French.

In April, the family traveled to Philadelphia to retrieve their belongings that had been sent by ship. Manny was alone when a telegram arrived from Chava in Israel. Manny knew enough English to understand the devastating news: David Mandel, Yehudah's, last surviving brother, had died suddenly the previous day.

Eleven

The story of Rezső Kasztner does not end simply. Whether he was right in negotiating with Eichmann to rescue Jews is a moral dilemma, one strongly argued even today. It is undeniable, however, that he did save lives, including Manny and his mother.

Kasztner survived the war and moved to Tel Aviv. By all accounts, urbane and smart, he soon became active in Mapai, the ruling political party of David Ben-Gurion and was given a government position. In the State of Israel he was also known as Israel Kastner.

In 1953, a Hungarian-born Israeli, Malchiel Gruenwald, published a little-read pamphlet accusing Kasztner, in a most broad and vicious manner, of being a collaborator with the Nazis, complicit in the Holocaust.

Inclined to let the matter fade, Kasztner did nothing. However, leading figures in Mapai were worried that the accusation would reflect badly on the party and the nation. They pushed for a libel action against Gruenwald. The trial began in January 1954.

Kasztner's testimony, the first of the trial, went well as he explained how he had negotiated with Eichmann and other Nazis. The Judge asked Gruenwald to withdraw his accusations, but he stubbornly said no.

The defense council was Shmuel Tamir, a forceful political opponent of Mapai. He confronted Kasztner antagonistically. "What happened to the Hungarian Jews sent to Auschwitz," he asked. "Why hadn't he warned them? Had he received special privileges?" And so on.

It seems surprising but for many in Israel, it was the first time they heard, in public, details about the horrors of the Holocaust.

By the time Judge Benjamin Halevi issued his ruling nine months after the trial ended in June 1955, there was no doubt how damaging the trial was to Kasztner's reputation and the standing of Mapai—it was one of the issues that toppled the government of then Prime Minister Moshe Sharrett.

Halevi said the Kasztner had "sold his soul to Satan," acquitting Gruenwald of all the libel charges but one; that Kasztner had financially benefited from his dealings.

The trial had an effect on the young nation of Israel. Soon plans were underway for a more formally observed Holocaust remembrance and for the building of Yad Vashem, a national memorial to the victims.

The government appealed the verdict, but before a ruling could be handed down, Rezső Kasztner was assassinated in front of his home in Tel Aviv. Less than a year later, in 1958, the original case was overturned and Kasztner was largely exonerated. But even in the appeal, one judge dissented.

Consider Kasztner's predicament—whom to pick for the train—a consummate example of the distress of war. To do nothing would have avoided criticism; to deal with the Nazis to save 1,676 Jewish souls, cost Kasztner his honor, and his life.

In 1960, Adolf Eichmann was captured in Argentina and secretly flown to Israel. This afforded the State of Israel and every other nation an opportunity to see the face of evil, confront one of the main architects of the murder of much of Europe's Jews and view the horrific apparatus of the Nazi killing machine.

Testimony was gathered, and depositions taken from witnesses around the world, in preparation for a trial which began in February 1961. It was presided over by three judges, Chief Judge Moshe Landau, Yitzhak Raveh and Benjamin Halevy, who was the judge in the Kasztner libel case.

Gideon Hausner, Israel's Attorney General delivered the opening remarks, saying about Eichmann:

"In this trial we shall encounter a new kind of killer, the kind that exercises his bloody craft behind a desk, and only occasionally does the deed with his own hands. Indeed we know of only one incident in which Adolf Eichmann actually beat to death a Jewish boy, who had dared to steal fruit from a peach tree in the yard of his Budapest home. But it was his word that put gas chambers into action; he lifted the telephone, railway trains left for the extermination centres; his signature sealed the doom of thousands and tens of thousands."

Journalist and author, Robert St. John, whose thinly disguised account of Kasztner, *The Man who Played God,* would be published the following year was in the courtroom along with hundreds of journalists, historians, and writers for newspapers, television, and radio. He sat slightly to the right of center, no more than twenty feet from Eichmann, who was in his bullet-proof glass cage, He described Eichmann, dressed in a dark suit with a handkerchief in its pocket, a white shirt and a tie.

"Sometimes," wrote St. John, "he toyed with a pencil. Sometimes he nervously adjusted the earphones through which he could hear a translation into German of everything that was said by judges, prosecutor or witness. Sometimes he scribbled a few words on a note pad. Sometimes he actually looked bored.

"He seemed more like an owner of a little grocery store somewhere, than the arch-criminal of all times. He also looked like a small-time bureaucrat."

One witness "became so hysterical when her turn came to testify that she started screaming in a high-pitched voice which unnerved almost everyone in that auditorium-courtroom. Yet Eichmann sat there with the fingers of his left hand on his chin, looking only mildly interested."

Eichmann justified his actions, claiming that he was just following orders. But it was shown that he was the primary force behind the deportations and liquidations of the Jewish population, especially in Hungary.

The case drew to a close during the last week of July. On the eight of August, the summation of the trial took place. On December 11, the court had its final word; guilty! It had been eight months since the proceedings began. Eichmann's execution was carried out at the end of the following May and his ashes spread into the Mediterranean.

Epilogue

Z vi and Ella took off from a former British military airport in Haifa, Israel, in a DC-3 two-engine prop plane, first landing in Egypt. From there, they flew to Tunis, to Nice and on to Brussels where they spent the day. Ella took time, like many who visit Brussels, to buy some lace. A Sabena Airlines Constellation flew them to Shannon, Ireland, where they were delayed for several hours while the plane's radio was repaired. They continued on their flight to New York with a stop in Gander, Newfoundland. At Idlewild Airport, they met Yehudah and from there the reunited family went to New York's Penn Station to board the train to Philadelphia.

Yehuda's sister, Helen, and her husband Barney Borish lived in a three-bedroom, one bath, row house (there was a toilet and slop sink in the basement), in Philadelpia's Strawberry Mansion neighborhood. They remained there for nearly ten days, until moving to New York City to a one bedroom apartment on the top floor at 72 Barrow Street in Greenwich Village.

Rabbi Chaim Porilla of Shaarey Shomayim Synagogue had

encouraged his congregation to sponsor Cantor Mandel's immigration. While Yehudah never had held specifically "rabbinic" employment, Porilla's congregation agreed to appoint him as their Associate Rabbi. This made his immigration status legal and the process smooth. All he had to do to enter the United States permanently was travel to Canada, exchange his visitor's Visa for a residential Visa and return to the United States. He did this at Niagara Falls.

In May of his first year in America, Manny, as Zvi became known, celebrated his bar mitzvah in his father's synagogue. Among those witnessing the ceremony was Yehudah's friend, Moshe Koussevitzky, who according to some was, "one of the finest Chazzans, if not the finest who ever lived."

Reflecting on that day, Manny said, "It was not an elaborate ceremony; after services, we had a luncheon." And then he added, lifting his shoulders, shaking his head and smiling, "I received a Parker 51 fountain pen."

That same year, Yehudah officiated at the wedding of his niece Sivi to Bob Boory. It was Manny's first experience at a wedding.

Bob later recalled, "It was the first time I heard the great voice of Chazzan Mandel; he shook the blinds with his powerful voice." Bob went on to say, "Aunt Helen, my mother-in-law was one special lady. She had a heart of gold and would go out of her way to be helpful. She was the greatest cook in the world and dished out dinners for the holidays for the entire family. She was a hard-working lady who also was able to help her husband make cigars, the family business. She was so proud of her brother, Yehudah."

Manny needed to be enrolled in school in New York City. His father was interested in a private Jewish day school. However, because of the paltriness of Manny's English, the day school officials suggested he enter the third or fourth grade, even though he was thirteen and had received a seventh grade certificate in Israel. The principal of P.S. 3, a public school a block from their apartment, proposed a solution to Yehudah.

Manny would be allowed to enter the seventh grade and if he fulfilled those scholastic requirements he could continue on to the eighth. If not, he would redo the seventh. The principal also agreed that it would not be necessary for Manny to take the required Spanish or other language course. Instead, he would be given an additional study hall each day in order to improve his English.

Manny passed seventh grade and went on to the eighth at P.S. 3. When Yehudah moved his family to a different apartment across town, Manny continued attending P.S. 3, commuting by bus.

While Yehudah enjoyed his star status at Shaarey Shomay-in, where he was required to perform only on all holidays, some sabbaths and special occasions, he became concerned that the neighborhood, 11th Street and Second Avenue, was not the best

Ella , Yehudah and Manny (on his bike purchased for him in 1949) Philadelphia 1950.

location for his family. In 1950, he investigated other positions and soon permanently settled on a congregation in Philadelphia. He accepted a position as Cantor at Beth Judah of Logan. This was to become the position he occupied for the next thirty-five years.

In the first fourteen years of his life, Manny learned and used three different languages while living in four different countries and attending no less than seven schools. For the first time, the move to Philadelphia in 1950 did not require a language change nor a new country, just a new environment. His Americanization process there began to include new experiences.

On the July 4th, Manny remembers attending his first baseball game. Actually, it was two games, a double-header with the Phillies versus the Boston Braves. The pitchers for the Braves were the legendary Warren Spahn, who eventually won more games than any lefty in history, and Johnny Sain. A popular slogan for success that Braves fans recited was "Spahn and Sain and pray for rain." It was the surprising Phillies, however, known as the "Wiz Kids," that captured the National League Pennant.

Manny recalled playing a game in Israel that seemed to be a combination baseball and cricket. "You hit the person with the ball and ran to the bases."

Manny also attended a wrestling match accompanied by his cousins, Sivi and Bob Boory. The featured attraction was Carl Donald Bell, a member of the Mohawk Tribe in Canada who wrestled in full Indian dress as Chief Don Eagle.

Yehuda purchased his first car, a 1950 Ford. For the rest of his life, he would buy a car every ten years or so. He had one credit card for gas—Amoco. "When he drove, he either had his foot on the gas or the brake. He often hit the bumpers of other cars as well as curbs,"his grandson, David, recalls.

"He lived life in a fixed routine. Serving as a cantor gave

him a responsibility to God." David conjectured that his grandfather lived a life devoid of politics. sports or hobbies.

"As a child he had one pair of clothes. Later in life, he dressed differently for breakfast, for work and when he came home from work." Once Yehudah wanted to buy a new seersucker suit for spring or summer wear. He drove to Wannamaker's Department Store. Tongue firmly in cheek, David told him he should have gone to "Sears" for the seersucker.

A group titled "Beth Judah of Logan, Philadelphia" was first added to Facebook in 2009. In spite of the long passage of time, people still remembered. One person wrote, "Kol Nidre by Cantor Mandel—a life-changing experience." Another said, "I always remember Beth Judah and Cantor Mandel especially. I got to sing tunes that we learned from Cantor Mandel in the High Holiday Choir at Beth Judah."

Soon after the Beth Judah Facebook group was created, David joined. He posted a recording of Cantor Mandel's singing in his riveting voice accompanied by piano. The Facebook comments continued: "At every Seder that I lead, I tell people how your Grandfather explained the word 'b'farech' (hard labor) when we were studying Exodus by talking about WWII concentration camps,"one person wrote.

Another of his many admirers said: "I have a special place in my heart for your grandfather. He was my mentor from when I was 6 years old, just starting to sing, thru college, majoring in voice, and into my 30's. He used to tell me stories about his life in Italy, after the war. . ."

Still another person wrote: "I was remembering the excitement of anticipating Selichot services at Beth Judah, the Saturday night before Rosh Hashanah. The services started at midnight and I got to stay up and take part—in the choir with Cantor Mandel. . .It was my favorite music of the entire holiday season."

During one of his years at Beth Judah of Logan Synagogue, Ella gave Yehudah a surprise. It was like the diamond ring that he always admired on his colleague's finger, the dapper Cantor Linetsky at the Dohany Temple in Budapest. Yehudah wore the ring for a quarter of a century but gave it to Manny for his forty-ninth birthday in 1985; Manny has worn it every day since.

Yehudah became engaged in leadership positions in the local and national associations of Cantors. He became President of the Cantors Assembly of the United Synagogue of America in 1970, and remained in that position for two years. The whole family attended his installation.

Anytime he came to sing before the group, the auditorium was filled with enthusiastic admirers.

In Philadelphia, Manny completed eighth grade at Jay Cooke Junior High School. At that time, the school system in Philadelphia permitted ninth grade to take place in either junior high school or high school. For ninth grade, all of Manny's friends chose to attend Central High School but he was asked to stay in Cooke because the counselor thought that this newly arrived boy would do better staying where he was.

Later, this delay was discovered to have been a mistake. Central was the first of the magnet system where, upon passing an entrance examination, a student could attend the school from anywhere in the city without zone or neighborhood restriction. Manny later realized that the school not only had his friends, but also a tradition and an approach that he found difficult to quickly grasp a year after his friends had started.

It took time to catch up. Central was an all-male public high school at that time. It was and still is noted for its high academic standards. Founded in 1836, it remains the second oldest high school in the United States. It is the only high school in the nation authorized to grant its graduates Bachelor of Arts degrees instead of ordinary high school diplomas. At one time, that degree gave students up to a two-year advanced placement at schools such as the University of Pennsylvania. Most alumni still remember the words of the school song and continue to sing and stomp their feet after the first and fifth line of the chorus:

> Let others sing of college days their Alma Mater true,
> But when we raise our voices, tis only High for you.
> We'll ne'er forget those days gone by, those glorious days of old,
> When oft we sang the praises of the Crimson and the Gold.
> Chorus: Dear high, dear Central High,
> Thy mem'ries never die.
> Thy honor we'll cherish and
> Laud it to the sky.
> On ballfield or in life,
> In peace or deadly strife, For thee we all will labor,
> For thee, oh dear old High!

Forging lifelong friendships, Manny met Bill Gottfried and Mort Kafrissen; they lived across the street from one another on the 4900 block of Ninth Street in the Logan section, a few homes

Ella, Yehudah and Manny in front of their home on 9th Street in Philadelphia, 1951.

from the Mandels at 4946. Manny and Bill became addicted to Charlie Chan movies, which they often watched on weekends.

Bill spent many enjoyable days at Manny's home with his parents, whom he described as "warm, welcoming and tight knit."

"Manny's mom made the best rice knishes." Bill said, "That taste remains with me to this day."

When they started tenth grade together, Manny, Bill and Mort walked to Central from their homes which were about fifteen blocks from school. They walked in the deep snows of winter and the heat of summer, always discussing and often planning their lives ahead. Rarely, in terrible weather, a parent of one of the boys would drive them. The only other option was public transportation, which entailed taking a bus, a subway and also a trolley in order to reach Central.

Though an average of three years younger than his fellow students, Manny held a major advantage over most at Philadelphia's Gratz College, a Hebrew teacher's institute. He was already fluent in Hebrew.

"I went there in the evenings, three nights a week." In 1953, he received a diploma.

Manny and Ella were both naturalized as U.S. citizens in 1954, though not together. A few years later, Adrienne, Manny's future wife, queried him about the "green" card he carried before becoming a U.S. citizen. Manny replied: "I was from a place called Permarez," which was his way of deflecting further inquiry. "It came from a "Permanent Resident" card I carried prior to becoming an American citizen." At the time it ended the discussion.

Manny, now eighteen, went to U.S. District Court VI in Philadelphia, on December 3, 1954, to take the citizen oath. Earlier in the day he had to answer basic questions, e.g., "What is the highest court in the United States?" He vividly recalls two fellow applicants at the ceremony, both wearing U.S. army uniforms; they were required to renounce their loyalty status to Czechoslovakia, their native country.

Yehudah's frequent forced labor battalion absences—sometimes for months—had to have seriously impacted Manny's sense of security. There would be no traditional nuclear family offering him sanctuary during these formative years. Manny was again separated from his father during his six months in Bergen-Belsen, another eight months while in Switzerland, and nearly a year when he lived in *Shaar HaAmakim* in Palestine, though Lajos, after a brief stay at the kibbutz, eventually brought his family together in Haifa. The uncertainty, the fear, the paternal absence before the family was finally reunited, no doubt, took its psychological toll. Manny takes issue with this notion: "Of course I missed my father, but labor camp was considered de rigueur — —as far as I was concerned, it was the nature of the world."

He remains particularly beholden to his mother. For over two years Ella functioned as mother and father. For over two years neither wife nor son knew the fate of husband and father, Oberkantor Lajos Mandel. During that time, Manny's relationship with his father was held in abeyance, in a state of ambiguous limbo. True, Manny's uncle, Lajos's younger brother, Dezso, oftentimes served as a kind of stand-in father, a hero figure if you will, a mentor of sorts, but often, he too went off with his peers, leaving Manny to fend for himself. Not to have been markedly traumatized after those years of fear, absence and uncertainty is a testament to Manny's inner strength.

Mort recalls that "Manny had a heavy accent in those days. One of his regular phrases was, 'Vell I tell you.'

Manny played on the Central High Varsity soccer team, and I was the manager of that team. In those days everyone in soccer had a thick accent because the best players came from [other] countries." Mort said this was why he wasn't thrown off kilter by Manny's foreign accent.

Tossing out a zinger, Mort also wrote that Manny's favorite book was *Prisoner of Zenda*. "He used this one time reading as the basis of many reports for different English classes."

Years later, Cantor Mandel presided at Mort's wedding at the Warwick Hotel in center city, Philadelphia. Yehudah "walked down the aisle singing as he came in."

Yehudah was also at the helm of Bill Gottfried's wedding in Brooklyn. "Cantor Mandel's voice was strong and warm. He sang in the traditional Ashkenazi style, with such verve and voice that it provided a foundation to Toby's and my marriage."

Manny reflected upon the formative years of his education: "I blame the Nazis for screwing up twelve years of my schooling." Upon graduation, Manny thought perhaps he might want to become either an electrical or a mechanical engineer "because it was something that required tinkering—I thought engineers fixed things, and I would like that." Later, he came to realize that he had other interests, other aptitudes.

Manny enrolled in a liberal arts program at Penn State University, at the university's Ogontz Center in Philadelphia. "It had been the Ogontz School for Girls. It was a beautiful campus with a duck pond, a gazebo, and four hundred kids. I was away from home all day."

He took one engineering course, and the usual core subjects—English, Math, and Psychology. At the end of two years, he could have continued, but, were he to stay at Penn State, he would have been required to move to the main campus in University Park; he wanted to remain in Philadelphia, where he was earning as much as many of his friends, teaching Hebrew school ten hours a week —from four to six every day, and from ten to twelve on Sunday.

"For those two years at the Ogontz Center, I was in Army ROTC; it was mandatory. In my second year, I was a platoon leader, Lieutenant Mandel. WWII British insignias and uniforms designated us; we wore no greens, but WW II olive drab. We carried M1's and we also had 45's with the firing pins removed."

In 1952 or 1953, Manny met his future wife, Adrienne Abramson from Hillside, New Jersey. At the time, he was in the Raymond Rosen AZA (Aleph Zadik Aleph) fraternity, and she was a member of BBG (B'nai B'rith Girls); in 1944, both groups had combined into the B'nai B'rith Youth Organization (BBYO). In BBG, Adrienne was the president of District III, representing four states, and was attending a convention in Philadelphia. Her train arrived late; Manny met her at the station with Adrienne's friend, Rochelle and her boyfriend, Dewey. A friendship blossomed; Manny and Adrienne often wrote to each other, the most common way of communicating from a distance in those days.

As twenty-year-old staff members, both attended a convention at Camp Akiba in the Pocono's. While there, Manny and Adrienne sat and talked and talked. At the time, Adrienne was a student at Rutgers; in 1958 she earned her B.A. in political science. In 1984, she received her M.A. from George Washington University in legislative policy. Nineteen years later (2003) she completed an Executive Program at the John F. Kennedy School of Government, Harvard University.

Manny had received a University Scholarship to attend a Seminar in Asian Life Studies at Temple University. He was to graduate from the experimental liberal arts program located at Temple the following year with a Bachelor of Education, a science degree. "I was now prepared for either a teaching career or graduate studies in social services. Clearly I wanted to be in people's lives, and help them." When asked if this self-awareness had anything to do with his experience in Europe, he said, "Yes, perhaps there is some connection there."

Manny and Adrienne started dating in June 1956. The following year Adrienne was leading a group of twenty-five young adults from the National Student Association; their destination Europe. Manny was also heading to Europe; on the continent, he planned to end in Naples where he would then set sail for Haifa. Before leaving for overseas, Manny's parents invited three of his friends, including Adrienne, for *Pesach* (Passover) At the *Seder*, Manny's Aunt Helen her children and grandchildren and two close friends were also there. Adrienne recalled, "They were truly scrutinizing me."

Adrienne, Rochelle Bakove, Bill Kaplan, Roberta Kaplan, Mort Kafsrissen, and Bill Gottfried saw Manny off at the dock in Hoboken. Adrienne and Manny had agreed to meet in Venice, which they did, spending three days together. Manny returned to the States first, and a few weeks later met with Adrienne again when she arrived home. He drove his father's car from Philadelphia to the Hoboken dock.

That Thanksgiving, Manny was invited to Adrienne's house for dinner. Unlike the Mandels, Adrienne's parents did not keep a kosher home, but Adrienne's grandmother lived with Adrienne's parents; she was familiar with the Hungarian language. Rounding out the family dinner were Adrienne's great-aunt on her mother's side and her husband, both of whom spoke fluent Hungarian.

Manny knew a local jeweler who lent him six "engagement rings" for Adrienne's perusal. She selected one. On November 15, 1958, one hundred fifty guests attended their wedding and sit-down dinner at a catering hall in nearby Maplewood, New Jersey. Future pediatrician, Bill Gottfried was Manny's best man; Rhoda Alper was Adrienne's maid of honor.

For four months, the newlyweds lived with Manny's parents. They remained there until Manny decided where he would attend grad school. Adrienne describes that it was a close-knit family, though not a demonstrative one—they were not publicly affectionate or physically demonstrative.

"They were more proper. Yehudah always dressed formally, even when he was helping Ella by sweeping off the front porch of their home wearing a half apron."

Obviously proud of Manny's accomplishments, Manny's parents treated Adrienne warmly. Ella spoke Hungarian to her Hungarian friends, while Lajos invariably communicated in English. Usually easy going, Yehudah would on occasion express himself quite sternly in words when something or someone disappointed or angered him.

The following year, 1959, Manny was awarded a Richard Klutznick Fellowship at the Graduate School of Social Work, University of Pennsylvania.

Manny and Adrienne's daughter, Lisa, was born in 1960. She is a graduate of the University of Michigan and The Columbia College of Law, Catholic University of America. After passing the Bar, Lisa Mandel Trupp became chief-of-staff to Montgomery County, Maryland Councilmember Phil Andrews. Sixteen years later, when Andrews ran for county office he had to vacate the seat and his successor, Sidney Katz, chose to retain Lisa.

"My grandmother passed away when I was seven," but from what Lisa can remember, "Both of my grandparents were kind, loving people—in a much different way than my father. My father is also a kind, loving person, but he does not really show this." *Gemutlichkeit*, Manny is capable of concealing. However there is a sparkle in his eyes, an all-knowing countenance. A man-of-the-world, Manny has little difficulty conversing with strangers. His memory of people, places and things is legion.

Lisa never heard her grandparents talk about the war, but points out that "My father talks about it freely although (only in the past twenty years or so—nothing before)." But here's the

The Klein sisters. Ilona, Magda, and Ella. Israel, 1957.

rub: "I think he speaks openly and honestly, but sometimes too glibly—almost making light of events and situations that I feel should never be made light of."

"Our horror and outrage seem to have eased, if not lessened. Auschwitz, Treblinka, Majdanek, Bergen-Belsen, Babi Yar, the Warsaw Ghetto. Gas chambers, selections, partisans, yellow Stars of David, crematories, mass-graves. . ." In an article about Holocaust remembrance entitled "Preserving the Mystery" for the *Forward*, Menachem Rosensaft wrote these words twenty years ago. This is about the time, Lisa suggests, that her father finally opened up about his experiences in the war.

She speaks of Manny's aunts as "stately women." There is a photograph of Ella with her two sisters, Magda and Ilona. Indeed they are stately women—tall, slender, with lush hair— beautiful.

Lisa feels herself fortunate to have heard her grandfather sing many times. "He took such pride in his ability, and that comes through in every note that he sang. His passion for his profession was evident and his abilities were tremendous." This description of Lajos' fervent emotion and privileged proficiency for his cantorial ability is shared, in similar words, by many others.

At the Rumbach Synagogue, Lajos Mandel had reached success at a very young age. He knew he was good; after the war he wasn't about to take up a new career. To him singing was like a craft—like woodworking, improving over time. As a musician, his voice was his instrument. Every day he practiced singing in private up until he reached the age of eight five. As he grew older, he modified his voice to compensate for his age. Naturally a physically strong man, many aches could probably be attributed to his time working as a forced laborer. Certainly he carried some pain with him most of his life, though he never talked about it.

Manny and Adrienne's son, David, was born in 1963. After attending Syracuse University, he has become an entrepreneur—and something of a bon vivant. "Work is not who I am; it's how I support myself." He is a fiercely independent thinker: "I've tried to avoid the butterfly effect where others influence your own decisions."

Over the years, David has helped organize and run several businesses—in television production, as service manager for BMW and Mercedes Benz—then helping to expand a company called Liberty Lock and Security Inc.; starting out with three employees, they ended up with thirty before he sold his share to his partner and good friend. Currently David is the owner of Alarm System Testing & Inspections, Inc.

With a smile broadening his bearded face, David recalls the weekends his grandfather spent preparing him for his

Manny, Detroit, 1972.

bar mitzvah. "He showed his disappointment when I didn't call to stay in touch with him. Both he and my dad were even and calm—not touchy-feely individuals. Granddad wanted my father and me to be menschen." Manny went in his own direction, David his.

Manny's professional training was at the Graduate School of Social Work of the University of Pennsylvania. Receiving his MSW in 1961, with enthusiasm, he adopted the Functional Method pioneered by the school. For fifteen years in his career of group work, administrative social work and counseling, Manny was able to do additional training that eventually prepared him for an independent practice as a psychotherapist where he was able to live up to his self-description as a "mental health provider."

Yehudah, with wife Lilly and Manny, after his election as president of the United Synagogue Cantor's Assembly, 1972.

Lisa, Adrienne, Manny, David 1983.

Manny's career resembles a graph in the bull market, a jagged but continually ascending line.

In 1961, Manny assumed the assistant directorship of the Ohio Region of the B'nai B'rith Youth Organization (BBYO). He was fulfilling a two year employment commitment made, a requirement of graduate school scholarship. In 1963, he was promoted to become the BBYO Director for the Michigan Region; in 1972, he was appointed national program director. This was his ticket to Washington D.C.. Various adjunct and concurrent employment opportunities occurred during his full time career in BBYO.

Between 1967 and 1972, at Wayne State University in Detroit, Manny was a university adjunct instructor. In 1968, Manny became a field instructor at the University of Michigan School of Social Work. Two years later saw him at Park Community Hospital in Detroit where he served as a consultant in Clinical Social Work. Between 1971 and 1972 he was a consultant in Geriatric Services at Petoskey Hall in Detroit.

Manny continued his BBYO employment, relocating his family

to Washington in 1973. After leaving that organization, he served as Executive Officer of a community based federally funded program in Southeast Washington. The years 1976-1984 saw Manny with the U.S. Peace Corps as a Training Officer. He developed plans and procedures in methods and models of staff training in areas of management, administration, planning, supervision and communication. He designed and delivered the human behavior segment for Peace Corps training to staff officers prior to their departure for overseas assignments.

From 1983, he was a Clinical Psychiatric Social Worker, initially part time and later full time, at the Roundhouse Square Psychiatric Center in Alexandria, Virginia. He provided cognitive therapy to adolescents and families in this multidisciplinary outpatient facility.

This experience solidified his decision to enter private practice in 1985. Seeing patients in both Maryland and Virginia, Manny maintained his practice for the rest of his career, retiring in 2014. He treated adults, adolescents and also conducted family therapy. "I deal mostly with mental health, not pathology. I treat depression and other dysfunctional issues. A parent might come to me and say, 'My teenage, high school senior son says he's leaving home-running away.' If I can help the family clarify their communication, have the son stay home through his senior year and then go away to college in the fall, I have helped the family and have done my job."

Patients mostly came to Manny from insurance listings, the Yellow Pages and referrals from extended families. He steadfastly adhered to a policy of having no contact with former patients or their families except for cases where a parent might call and say, "You saw my son, would you see my daughter."

Manny has always been a consummate professional and this is also reflected in his community activities. Four Maryland governors have taken advantage of his expertise.

Governor Harry Hughes appointed him to a Gubernatorial Task Force which dealt with child, teenage and young adult suicide and other mental health problems. Manny participated in drafting the final report. The Mental Hygiene Administration incorporated many of his recommendations and put them into practice. Governor Donald Schafer confirmed Manny's appointment to a Governor's Task Force that studied Health Professional Client Sexual Exploitation. Governor Parris Glendenning appointed Manny, and Governor Robert Ehrlich reappointed him, to the Maryland Board of Social Work Examiners, the license granting entity for Social Workers in the state. He served for eight years with two as Chair.

Adrienne Mandel, a Democrat, was elected to the Maryland General Assembly in 1994 representing Maryland Legislative District 19. She served as a Delegate for twelve years, was elected President of The Women's Legislators of Maryland and was chief sponsor of significant highway safety and senor health care laws. After retiring from the House of Delegates, Adrienne was appointed by County Executive Isiah Leggett to serve as a Commissioner of the bi-county Washington Suburban Sanitary Commission (WSSC). She served for eight years, twice as Chair.

Manny and Adrienne traveled the United States and abroad. The first of these trips, in 1969, was when Manny returned to Israel for the third time but this time with Adrienne, nine year old Lisa, six year old David and Adrienne's recently widowed mother, Florence Abramson.

Manny reveals that the children wondered why we did not have a tour name as so many others. So the legend of IMI Tours was created and exists to this day when the family travels together.

This Israel trip, lasting about five weeks, had the family driving all over the country in a Volkswagen. The German vehicle may seem like a strange choice for Manny, but like many

Holocaust survivors he harbors little negative feeling; the Germans of today are not the Germans of the war. Manny says: "Ben Gurion could deal with the Germans in trade and reparations, so can I." They visited Haifa, including the Bahai's World Center, Jerusalem, the Golan Heights, Masada in the Sinai, and the Shalom tower, at the time the tallest building in the Middle East. This trip was also a welcome opportunity for Manny's immediate family to get to know his Israeli family.

Adrienne and Manny have enjoyed many other travels, including a number of U.S. National Parks, the Caribbean, South America, much of Europe, China, South East Asia, and Australia and New Zealand.

A memorable trip for Manny occurred in 2009 when his son David took him to Israel, ostensibly to participate in the wedding of a cousin from his mother's side of the family.

Manny's cousin, Avraham Shaked, the son of the youngest Mandel brother, David, who was in Bergen-Belsen with Manny,

Manny Mandel 2008.

was asked to guide them on a special excursion. Shaked is Hebrew for Mandel, "almonds" in German. This surname was adopted by Manny's uncle David upon his arrival in Palestine in 1945.

Avraham, at one time a very free soul, sometimes described himself as an "inactive anarchist." He spent several years as the Director of the Field School at the Montastero di Santa Caterina near Mt. Sinai and is considered one of the world's experts on the Sinai; Manny requested that they climb to the top of the mountain where Moses received the Ten Commandments. The three men rode camels part of the way and then had to climb the rest.

While climbing Manny's legs started to cramp up. "Dad does not complain about physical pain," said David. Manny sat on a rock to rest. Avraham told Manny that twenty-five years prior, his father, Yehudah, had been escorted on a similar trip and he, too, didn't get to the top. "I think he sat on the same rock," said Avraham. The two younger men reached the top of the mountain with an overwhelming feeling of joy at their accomplishment. Then they came back for Manny and slowly walked him to the top.

In December 1967, shortly before her sixtieth birthday Ella Mandel died. She had developed an inoperable tumor. After thirty seven years, Yehudah was alone. Within a year, mutual friends introduced him to Lilly Miklos. She and her husband had emigrated to the United States from Hungary during the upheaval of the 1956 Hungarian Revolution. Like Yehudah, both of them were Holocaust survivors. After a long illness, in 1968, Lilly's husband passed away. Lilly and Yehudah married in 1969 and were together for the next twenty-four-plus years. Yehudah died in 1994, just shy of his ninetieth birthday. Lilly died in 2008. At her funeral Manny offered his appreciation: "She gave my father twenty-five wonderful years."

Manny gave an oral history for the United States Holocaust Memorial Museum in 1989. When asked why he testified, Manny said: "It's incredibly important. As George Santayana pointed out, if you don't learn your history well, you may relive it. It, the war, was not a docudrama. It was real, and ought to be gathered from live testimony,"

The following year, Manny made arrangements for Yehudah to give his version of events to the same organization. In looking at the tape, one sees a perfectly round face, dark eyebrows, a ski nose, gray hair, and an ingratiating smile. Yehudah was broad shouldered, powerful in appearance. He was obviously intelligent, shrewd, and articulate and, for a man of eighty-five, possessed a keen memory. He was patient and pleasant with the interviewer, who periodically interrupted him to lead the discussion into other areas.

In 1997, Manny gave another oral history, this time to the Survivors of the Shoah Visual History Foundation. Bright, quick on the uptake, and articulate, Manny spoke with a rapid, rat-a-tat clip to his sentences; one can detect an ever so slight Hungarian accent. His interests are catholic; he has a residue of facts and life experiences at his fingertips, and is not hesitant to express his stance on any number of issues—politics is in his blood; he is a registered Democrat, though he has, on occasion, voted for an individual of the other major party. When asked who his favorite president is, without hesitation Manny says, "Harry Truman." Then, with a wink, he lets you know they share the same birthday, May 8.

Manny's once dark brown hair is thinning and graying. Still, at five-foot-ten and weighing 185 pounds, he remains solidly built. A kind person, he has a handsome physiognomy, a ruddy healthy-looking complexion, an erect posture, an affable smile, and is generally upbeat.

When asked if he had it to do all over again, what would

he change about his life? "I would have learned how to play the piano," a point he had brought up previously..

Manny doesn't suffer fools, but he is adept at masking his inner feelings, often resorting to his droll sense of humor. He was once asked at the Holocaust Museum: "How did you survive the Holocaust?" He answered: "They didn't kill me."

However, let us not forget, while being incarcerated for six months in Bergen-Belsen, every day he faced fear, intimidation, humiliation and disease—and in due course he and his fellow Jews suffered from starvation.

The family Mandel experienced much privation, fear and terror at the hands of mankind's lesser angels. Nonetheless, they have contributed a great deal to both the privileged and needy, most of whom have lived comparatively secure and sheltered lives. It has indeed been a lifetime in the days of the Family Mandel. May they all live to be one hundred twenty!

Remarks by Dr. Emanuel Mandel on behalf of the World Federation of Bergen-Belsen Associates Bergen-Belsen, April 26, 2015

President Gauck, Prime Minister Weil, President Lauder, Ladies and Gentlemen,

I am Manny Mandel from Washington, D.C.

On this day of commemoration I bring you greetings from the President of the World Federation of Bergen-Belsen Associates, my friend Sam Bloch of New York City, who is unable to be here in person, but asked that I speak on his behalf.

My memories of this place are those of an eight-year-old boy who arrived here in July 1944 as part of the Kasztner train of transport. We were told that this would be a three-day rest and recuperation stop prior to boarding ships for our journey away from Europe as part of the Nazi plan to make Europe *Judenrein*. Three hundred and fifty of the seventeen hundred members of the group were released to Switzerland after some six weeks. I was not among them and spent much of that fall through December in Barrack 10 in the Hungarian camp. The negotiations continued and later in the year we, too, were transported to Switzerland. We became free before the end of the war and before Bergen-Belsen turned into the horror camp it became in the winter and early spring of 1945.

We have just celebrated Pesach, the Jewish festival of Passover. And in the spirit of that holiday we, today, also remember: "*Mitzvah Aleinu lesaper b'yetziat ha-Shoah v'chol shemarbe lesaper b'yetziat ha-Shoah harey ze meshubach*—it is our obligation to tell the story of our emergence from the fires of the Holocaust and all who expand on this experience of ours are to be praised."

We remember the seventy years and more of all that Bergen-Belsen and its history placed in our lives. We remember and retell of our arrival at the train platforms some short distance from here, our forced march to the barracks whose only remaining physical evidence are some foundation stones not bulldozed and not burned upon liberation. We remember and retell of the daily, lengthy Appell that kept us standing for hours in the rain, the mud and the cold.

Above all we remember those who lie here in mass graves whose final dignity is denied and are memorialized by a number such as "here lie 5,000". While Bergen-Belsen did not become a killing camp such as Auschwitz, it was nonetheless a death camp. The malnutrition, starvation, the dreaded and untreatable typhus were the Zyklon-B pellets of this place. Nowhere else did the liberating forces find the emaciation seen here and described by the British physicians, commanders and clergy when they entered this place.

And yet life came after death. The Bergen-Belsen Displaced Persons camp that was a transitional home for many for five years, until 1950, was the place where over two thousand Jewish children were born, some of whom are here today. Among them is Menachem Rosensaft, the son of Josef Rosensaft, the leader of the survivors of Bergen-Belsen throughout the DP years.

This place of death mandates that we etch into our memory banks the concept of George Santayana who spoke of remembering the past so we can mitigate against it happening again.

We wonder whether the world has learned enough of the past to avoid repetition and therefore our task today is to remember and commemorate with those who are with us today and those who are not, whether they lie here or in all the other places where the Nazis, *yemach shemam*, may their name be cursed, practiced their horrid tasks.

As many survivors say today: standing on the ashes of the millions who were annihilated, we embody the legacy of the Holocaust. The courage and dignity of the survivors shed a bright light on our children and grandchildren who by their very existence defy the "final solution to the Jewish question" as enunciated at the Wannsee conference in Berlin in 1942.

To paraphrase the words of Abraham Lincoln, we *are* here to dedicate and consecrate this hallowed ground to our brethren, parents and others in whose memory we stand here and, at the appropriate time, we will together say Kaddish, the memorial prayer for our dead.

Selected Bibliography

Defoe, Daniel. *Robinson Crusoe élete és kalandjai.* Translated by Radó Antal. Budapest: Lampel Róbert (Wodianer F. és fiai), 1909.

Dubnow, S. M. *History of the Jews in Russia and Poland: From the Earliest Times until the Present Day.* Philadelphia: The Jewish Publication Society of America, 1916.

Eban, Abba. *Introduction to Hannah Senesh: Her Life & Diary.* New York: Schocken Books, 1972.

Elon, Amos. *The Israelis: Founders and Sons.* New York: Holt, Rinehart and Winston, 1971.

———. *Timetable: The Story of Joel Brand.* London: Hutchinson, 1981.

Encyclopedia Judaica. Jerusalem: *Encyclopedia Judaica,* 1972.

Esbenshade, Richard S. *Hungary: Cultures of the World.* New York: Marshall Cavendish, 2005.

Gilbert, Martin. *Atlas of the Holocaust.* New York: William Morrow Company, Inc., 1993.

———. The Holocaust: *A History of the Jews of Europe during the Second World War.* New York: Henry Holt and Company, 1985.

Grosser, Paul E., and Edwin G. Halperin. *The Causes and Effects of Anti-Semitism: The Dimensions of a Prejudice: An Analysis and Chronology of 1,900 Years of Anti-Semitic Attitudes and Practices.* New York: Philosophical Library, 1978.

Harel, Isser. *The Truth about the Kasztner Murder: Jewish Terror in the State of Israel.* Jerusalem: Edanim, 1985.

Hausner, Gideon. *Justice in Jerusalem.* New York: Harper and Row, 1966.

Hebbert, Charles, Norm Longley, and Dan Richardson. *Hungary.* 5th ed. New York: Rough Guides, 2002.

Hecht, Ben. *Perfidy: The Kasztner Affair.* New York, Messner, 1961.

Horowitz, Terry Fred. *Merchant of Words: The Life of Robert St. John.* Lanham, MD: Rowman & Littlefield, 2014.

Kadar, Gabor, and Zoltan Vagi. *Self-financing Genocide: The Gold Train, the Becher Case, the Wealth of Jews,* Hungary. Budapest: Central European University Press, 2004.

Kershaw, Alex. *The Envoy: The Epic Rescue of the Last Jews of Europe in the Desperate Closing Month of World War II.* Cambridge, MA: Capo Press, Inc., 2010.

Ladany, Shaul. *King of the Road: From Bergen-Belsen to the Olympic Games.* Jerusalem: Gefen Publishing House, Ltd., 2008.

Learsi, Rufus. *Israel: A History of the Jewish People.* Cleveland: The World Publishing Company, 1949.

Lieber, Joseph S., and Christina Shea, with Erzsebet Barat. *Frommer's Budapest & the Best of Hungary, 5th edition.* Hoboken, NJ: Wiley Publishing, Inc., 1998.

Lob, Ladislaus, *Dealing with Satan: Rezso Kasztner's Daring Rescue Mission.* London: Jonathan Cape, 2008.

Margolis, Max L., and Alexander Marx. *A History of the Jewish People*. New York: Atheneum, 1977.

Morse, Arthur D. *While Six Million Died: A Chronicle of American Apathy*. New York: Random House, 1968.

Nicholson, Michael, and David Winner. *Raoul Wallenberg: The Swedish Diplomat Who Saved 100,000 Jews from the Nazi Holocaust before Mysteriously Disappearing*. Harrisburg, PA: Morehouse Publishing, 1989.

Orr, Akiva. "The Kastner Case, Jerusalem, 1955" in *Israel: Politics, Myths and Identity Crisis*. London: Pluto Press, 1994.

Porter, Anna. *Kasztner's Train: The True Story of Rezso Kasztner, Unknown Hero of the Holocaust*. Madeira Park, BC: Douglas and McIntyre, 2008.

Sachar, Howard M. *A History of the Jews in the Modern World*. New York: Alfred A. Knopf, 2005.

Schreiber, Mordecai, ed. *The Shengold Jewish Encyclopedia*. Rockville, MD: Shengold Publishers, 2007.

Shirer, William L. *The Rise and Fall of the Third Reich: A History of Nazi Germany*. New York: Simon and Schuster, 1960.

Slezkine, Yuri. *The Jewish Century*. Princeton, NJ: Princeton University Press, 2004.

Smith, Geddes. *American Diplomacy during the Second World War, 1941-1945*. New York: John Wiley & Sons, 1965.

Soros, Tivadar. *Masquerade: Dancing around Death in Nazi-Occupied Hungary*. New York: Arcade Publishing, 1965.

St. John, Robert. *The Man Who Played God: A novel about Hungary and Israel*. Garden City, New York: Doubleday & Company, Inc., 1962.

Stowe, Harriet Beecher. *Uncle Tom's Cabin*. Translated by Tamás bátya kunyhója, vagy Néger élet a rabszolgatartó Amerikai Államokban. Angolból Irinyi József. Pesten, Müller E. könyvymodája, 1853.

United States Holocaust Memorial Museum. n.d. *Holocaust Encyclopedia*. Washington, D.C.: United States Holocaust Museum (website). https://www.ushmm.org/learn/holocaust-encyclopedia.

Vagi, Zoltan. *The Holocaust in Hungary: Evolution of a Genocide*. Lanham, MD: AltaMira Press, 2013.

Wallenberg, Raoul. *Letters and Dispatches: 1924-1944*. New York: Arcade Publishing, 1995.

Weisberg, Alexander. *Desperate Mission*. Whitefish, MT: Kessinger Publishing, LLC, 1958.

Weitz, Yechiam. *The Man Who Was Murdered Twice: The Life, Trial and Death of Israel Kasztner*. Translated by Chaya Naor. Jerusalem: Yad Vashem, 2012.

Wyman, David S. *The Abandonment of the Jews*. New York: New Press, 1998.

Yahil, Leni. *The Holocaust: The Fate of European Jewry, 1932-1945*. New York: Oxford University Press, 1990.

Zeiger, Henry A. *The Case against Adolf Eichmann*, edited with a Commentary by Henry A. Zeiger. With a forward by Harry Golden. New York: The New American Library, 1960.

Zweig, Ronald W. *The Gold Train: The Destruction of the Jews and the Looting of Hungary*. New York: William Morrow, 2002.

Articles

Bilsky, Leora. "Judging Evil in the Trial of Kastner." Law and History Review 19.1 (Spring 2001): 117-160.

Fried, S. "In-Depth Features: The Kasztner Trial." Dei'ahvedibur Information & Insight. July 23 2003. http://www.chareidi.org/archives5763/MTS63features.htm

LeBor, Adam. "Eichmann's List: A Pact with the Devil." The Independent. August 22, 2000. http://www.independent.co.uk/news/world/europe/eichmanns-list-a-pact-with-the-devil-711468.html

Films

Gloomy Sunday. Directed by Rolf Schübel. Germany: Studio Hamburg Filmproduktion, 1999. DVD, 114 min.

Killing Kasztner. Directed by Gaylen Ross. USA: GR Films, 2012. DVD, 129 min.

Mishpat Kastner. Directed by Uri Barbash. Israel: Israel Broadcasting Authority, 1995. DVD, 180 min.